Rodchenko

German Karginov

Rodchenko

with 211 illustrations, 67 in colour

Thames and Hudson

Translated by Elisabeth Hoch

Designed by Simon Koppány

Colour photographs by Kirill Popov, Károly Szelényi
Black-and-white photographs by Alexander Rodchenko, Nikolai
Lavrentev, German Karginov and István Petrás

First published in Great Britain in 1979
by Thames and Hudson Ltd, London
Original edition published in Hungary
by Corvina Kiadó, Budapest

Printed and bound in Hungary
Zrinyi Printing House, Budapest 1979

CONTENTS

PART ONE

Introduction

At the end of the 1940s Alexander Rodchenko wrote a short study in which he paid tribute to a man he had met at the beginning of 1916, shortly before his own works first appeared in public at 'Magazin' ('The Store'), an exhibition staged by the Cubo-Futurists in Moscow. The friendship which followed this meeting played a decisive role in Rodchenko's life. The man he met was Vladimir Tatlin, and, according to Rodchenko, it was from this master that he 'acquired a respect for vocation, for objects and materials; in short, for life as a whole'.

Rodchenko can hardly have thought of publishing his article when he wrote it: the artistic outlook of the period made this quite impossible. Perhaps it was an awareness of impending old age that made him finally set pen to paper to ease the accumulated tension of his memories; the eyewitness of great events has a natural desire to speak of the things he has seen, heard and pondered over. Rodchenko wrote of Tatlin:

He is a powerful artist, a true Russian, who loves recognition, yet is able and prepared to wait. I feel certain that he will win it in due course. Only a true Russian artist can create with such great zeal, in simple and pure taste, for the unknown future, without receiving any recognition for years or even until his death.

When Rodchenko wrote these words, imbued with both hope and bitterness, Tatlin was still alive. So were Rodchenko's comrades and companions-in-arms with whom he had translated the rhythm and colours of the Revolution into novel, 'strictly constructed coloured compositions of three-dimensional planes' and, later, into posters, architectural designs and book jackets.

With these same comrades he had dreamt of a mysterious and beautiful country of the future, which they named 'Futuria', where life was to be governed by the laws of beauty and harmony. But they did more than day-dream: when circumstances required it, they left the confined premises of their art 'laboratories' to do productive work in factories, printing offices, the building industry and elsewhere. They did so, not because they wanted to lower the standard of fine arts to the level of manual work, but because they wished to raise the qualitative standards of production, to breathe into it new life and sense, and to bring it into harmony with the requirements of a century of technical, social and intellectual revolution. And it was no fault of theirs if their many plans and ideas – often daring but never escapist – were seldom realized. In fact not only did their dreams and plans soon fall into oblivion: their very persons were forgotten while they were still alive.

One of the most interesting chapters in the history of Soviet Russian – and of European – culture has been skimmed over too quickly and superficially. The pages believed to have been empty are now gradually being filled. Articles and comprehensive works dealing with the period in question are increasing in number, and the first monographs are appearing. As a result, the number of malicious or unintentional distortions of the past is declining; links between events are being reconstructed, and the life and work of the artists, poets and composers who gathered around the banner of the new art, over half a century ago, are being clarified. Sometimes even such simple facts as a place and date of birth, or the schooling of certain artists, still need clarification, even though the people in question are almost our contemporaries and were well-known personalities in their time, all of them living and working in major cultural centres. Take Rodchenko himself: he was not born in Kiev, nor did he study at the Odessa School of Arts, as certain works on modern art claim.

Rodchenko's family and childhood

Alexander Mikhailovich Rodchenko was born in St Petersburg (later called Petrograd, now Leningrad). His birth certificate provides the following data: 'Date of birth: 23 November 1891; christened Alexander on 1 December. Father: Mikhail Rodchenko, landless peasant from the Zhukovskaya zone of Viazemsky district in Smolensk province. Legitimate wife: Olga Yevdokimovna. Both adherents of the Eastern Church, and both married for the first time.'

The artist's mother came from a family of Old Believers in northern Russia.[1] They owned a glass-ware shop but became impoverished after the father's early death. In order to support the family, Olga's mother went out to work as a washerwoman, and Olga herself joined her later. The artist's father had a short but colourful life. Son of a one-time serf, Mikhail Rodchenko was born free and had the courage to make use of his freedom, for one day he left his father's house to seek his fortune. Alexander Rodchenko tells us in his autobiographical notes that his father started his career as a railway construction labourer: 'Advancing towards St Petersburg, he became more and more polished, and even learned to write a little with the help of his foreman.'

In the capital of the Empire Mikhail tried his hand at many jobs. He worked as an assistant in a confectioner's shop, as a road-sweeper, as a waiter, and later as a footman at the house of a young count who was in love with a café singer and eventually shot himself. He even acted as a life statue in a palace:

Powdered and dressed in thin tights, and equipped with shield, sword and halberd, they had to stand motionless at the banister of the front steps from an hour before the beginning of the ball until after it had ended. It was a well paid but extremely repugnant job: the ladies mocked them and teased them by fanning certain parts of their bodies, so that they had to cover themselves with their shields.

At the time of Alexander's birth his father reached the peak of his varied career:

I was born above the stage of a theatre. It was part of the Petersburg Russian Club in the Nevsky where, after many trials and tribulations, my father was working as property-man. . . .

Ever since I can remember, I have always felt a certain solitude. I can still recall wandering about in the empty rooms of the Russian Club, which in the early morning hours had not been cleaned up after the ball of the previous night. There was a mess of empty sweetmeat boxes, bits of paper, ribbons and streamers. . . .

We had no neighbours living near us. Our rooms above the stage were the only living quarters in the building. There was no one to visit and nothing to play with; besides, it was boring to play by myself. I sat on our sofa gazing into the lamp, but it was tedious, as if the light were spreading a sort of dreariness. I had to fall back on my own imagination: in the towel hanging on a nail, in a piece of bristle, I saw the outlines of dead bodies or monsters sitting in a dark corner.

I thought that the city consisted only of theatres like the one we lived in and that everywhere life was similar to ours. I had no idea that blocks of flats, factories, prisons, and even palaces existed.

Once my father took us to the circus. It amazed me so much that the circus has remained my favourite spectacle to this day. Everything was astonishing: everyday objects darted about, revolved and became transformed; men stood on their heads or hands and flew through the air. They wore fantastic glittering clothes.

Kazan and the School of Arts

Little is known of the artist's adolescence and youth. In his auto-biographical notes Rodchenko himself passes over them in silence. He probably had good reason for doing so. Son of a landless peasant and a washerwoman, he had neither exciting adventures nor experiences of travel. Even the right to secondary school education was disputed. In 1910, when he registered at the School of Arts at Kazan, 1500 miles east of St Petersburg, all Rodchenko could produce was an elementary parochial-school report card from 1905, the year he left school. With this certificate he was allowed to attend the art school only as a 'guest student'. However, sad as they were in themselves, these circumstances eventually stood Rodchenko in good stead, for they played a role in the development of his judgment of aesthetic values. The freedom of the guest-student status, and the comparatively liberal atmosphere of the Kazan School of Arts, were fertile ground for Rodchenko's natural gifts and receptive mind.

By the beginning of 1916 Rodchenko was to be a member of the avant-garde of Russian artists. The significance of this achievement can be fully assessed only if we consider the fact that modern Russian art was born essentially from the work and the aspirations of a group of individuals, the so-called Leftist youth,[2] who were mainly men of technical or classical education, members of the bourgeoisie or even of the aristocracy, hothouse products of the lively intellectual and cultural life of the two capitals. Many of them had also spent some time studying in Montmartre or Montparnasse and so helped introduce into Russia the new Parisian movements which formed the foundation of Russian avant-garde art.

By the time Rodchenko registered at the School of Arts in 1910, the process which was to lead to the formation of a relatively united block of young Leftist artists in Moscow and St Petersburg was approaching its final phase: the Youth Association (*Soyuz Molodiozhi*)[3] was already established, and preparations for the first Knave of Diamonds (*Bubovnii Valet*)[4] exhibition were in progress. The young painters were still under the influence of Cézanne, of Fauvism, and of Primitivism;[5] but while they were creating new variations of these styles for themselves, Cubism was increasingly in evidence. The poets had reached the threshold of Futurism with their volume entitled *The Garden of Judges* (*Sadok Sudei*),[6] published at the beginning of the year.

Kazan was not exactly behind the times, but one can safely say that the events of cultural life in Moscow and St Petersburg reached the distant banks of the Volga with less than the speed of an express or even a mail-coach. Although Rodchenko ranked among the progressive students fairly early, he was at least ten years behind the Moscow artists as far as 'Leftist' attitudes were concerned: 'In this remote region,' he wrote, 'our "Leftism" was rather relative. Nikitin and I, for example, although we were the most Leftist of all, still painted like Vrubel and Gauguin, as no art more Leftist in outlook than theirs had reached us.'

It would appear that not even copies of *Golden Fleece* (*Zolotoe Runo*)[7] or *Apollo* (*Apollon*)[8] were received by Rodchenko or his friends. Their models and sources of inspiration were the reproductions appearing in *World of Art* (*Mir Iskusstva*),[9] a review which popularized Russian and Western European Art Nouveau.

The works of Rodchenko's early student years show little trace of Gauguin's influence, but his panels and sketches produced between 1910 and 1912 have a definite relationship with Vrubel's graphic style. This is evident, for example, in his pencil drawing of 1910 entitled *In the Restaurant* [1]. Here the young Rodchenko zealously imitated one of the major characteristics of Vrubel's drawings, his twofold technique. This essentially consisted of first developing the basic forms with dense hatching and then using strong outlines to give final shape to the details.

For some time drawing played a secondary role in Rodchenko's art. He preferred painting, especially in bright, warm tones of red, yellow and ochre. His experiments with contrasting colours – blue and red, green and red, for example – also showed great promise. From 1912 onwards he regularly used silver, bronze and lacquer in his sketches, especially those in watercolour. At the same time his interest in black, which he treated as a colour, markedly increased.

Rodchenko's early works naturally show certain shortcomings in composition or drawing; but these are richly compensated for by the freshness and boldness of his ideas. The *Portrait of N. A. Rusakov*, 1912 [6], for example, is extremely daring both in technique and colour. Rodchenko did not lose his way in a dense mass of paint but worked with a sure touch in large, solid patches of green, black, red and yellow, which are laid on the basic form of the head with a palette knife. It should be mentioned here that the early development of Rodchenko's talent as a painter was due in no small measure to Nikolai Feshin, who taught at the Kazan School of Arts at that time and who was remembered by Rodchenko as 'a light in the darkness'.

The years 1912 and 1913 were particularly important to Rodchenko's further progress: it was then that he began to take an interest in Art Nouveau book illustrations, especially those of Aubrey Beardsley (who was fairly popular in Russia at the time), and in eastern motifs. Both *World of Art* (*Mir Iskusstva*), and a review entitled *Balance* (*Vesi*),[10] which was the most important press organ of the Symbolists, devoted considerable space to Beardsley's art. Probably, however, it was a collection of articles on the art of Aubrey Beardsley, issued by Skorpio Publishers in 1912, that gave direct impetus to the development of Rodchenko's new interest. This fascination with Beardsley resulted in Rodchenko's adoption of stylization, a mode in which he felt at home immediately, and which led him into the world of intricate patterning and the music of abstract linear rhythms.

Although Rodchenko's turn to stylization cannot be regarded as an entirely foregone conclusion, certain characteristics of his method of working had played a determining role in it. From the very beginning, Rodchenko seldom worked from nature. Even in the first months of his studies he often painted invented compositions, as we can see from the numerous studies and sketches that exist. The subjects which appear most frequently include the coffee-house, the restaurant, the ball and the theatre [1, 3, 5]. There are practically no still-lifes to be found among his works, and most of his landscapes and portraits are either fictitious or painted from memory. It is also clear that the narrative content of the subject and the emotions of the figures depicted were treated as of secondary significance. Rodchenko preferred theatrical and spectacular representations to literary ones. Some of his compositions seem to represent performances taking place in the imagination of the artist. He was engrossed with the creative process itself: with the autonomous development of form and colour [4]. In short, from the very beginning his creations were governed by the laws of a 'second nature', that of art. It was what he had observed in art that passed through the filter of his emotions and knowledge: he had already freed himself from the ballast of nature.

The artist reached the extremes of abstraction fairly rapidly. It suffices to compare *Woman* [7] with *Woman in Kimono* [8], both of which were produced in 1913. In the first drawing the stylization is fairly moderate except in the background, while in the second, apart from the head of the figure, we find ourselves in a mysterious world of dots, patches, lines and empty space. His *Landscape in Oriental Style* [10] is entirely abstract apart from the branches seen on the left side of the composition. The use of black and bronze dematerializes the individual forms of this painting, while the vigorous crossing of the diagonal lines with straight verticals renders the composition a bold one regardless of whether we consider it as a landscape or an abstract.

Rodchenko trained himself to think in abstract forms by creating *Label*, 1913 [9], and other similar drawings of and exercises with nonobjective decorative elements. This helped develop his sense of proportion and rhythm, and his mastery in the application of line. Stylization streng-thened the discipline of his working methods and at the same time kept his temperament in check. (Rodchenko mentions yet another, now untraceable drawing from 1913, entitled *Non-Object. Tempera and Bronze*.)

Towards the end of 1914 Rodchenko's interest in the non-objective world assumed well-defined outlines. We must emphasize, however, that unlike Larionov, who created Rayonism, Malevich, who created Suprematism, or Tatlin, who approached non-objective art from Cubism or Cubo-Futurism, Rodchenko reached the same position through the abstracting tendencies of Art Nouveau.

It is difficult to tell whether Rodchenko would ever have taken the final step into full abstraction without outside impetus. His youth, his inexperience, and especially his lack of suitable surroundings and live contact with the 'homeland of art', were conditions unfavourable to an even moderately 'Leftist' attitude. But an event which took place in Kazan on 20 February 1914 played a decisive role in forming Rodchenko's radical outlook. This was the Futurist lecture held in the council hall of the Nobles' Assembly, with the participation of David Burliuk, Vladimir Mayakovsky and Vassily Kamensky. These artists discussed the problems of modern art and read their own poems. Rodchenko, who was present, called the event 'the second most soul-stirring experience in my life' (the circus being the first). He was particularly fascinated by Mayakovsky's personality and performance. A contemporary police report says of Mayakovsky:

He appeared on the platform and declared: 'I am clever.' There was Homeric laughter in the rows of the audience but this did not seem to embarrass Mayakovsky in the least. He began his talk in which he tried to prove that beauty was not a category determined for ever.[11]

After this Mayakovsky read his poems: 'So I went up to the barber, and said I am the serene. Please comb my ears. . . .'

'Of course,' declared Rodchenko, 'I became not merely their admirer but their devoted follower.'

Moscow and 'The Store'

Rodchenko finished his studies at the Kazan School of Arts in 1914. From a practical standpoint, however, this meant nothing. The status of 'guest student' deprived him of the rights conferred by the school on its graduates. He enrolled at the Stroganov School of Applied Arts in Moscow with a view to studying graphic art.

Rodchenko arrived in Moscow in the spring or summer of 1915, but spent only a few months at the Stroganov School, as he soon found he could not learn what he wanted there. Despite difficult financial circumstances and a hopeless future, he decided to pursue painting openly, and as a 'Leftist' reformer at that, thus rendering his prospects doubly hopeless. Recalling this period he wrote:

I wore a single threadbare coat winter and summer, lived in a cubicle behind a kitchen stove from which I was separated only by some plywood panels, and I starved, the little I succeeded in earning going for paint to the last penny. Yet I held the bourgeoisie in contempt and despised their favoured art, as well as the aesthetes of the Association of Russian Artists and *Mir Iskusstva*.[12] Artists like Tatlin, Malevich, Mayakovsky, Khlebnikov and others who, like me, remained unappreciated, whose works did not sell, and who were damned by all the papers, were much closer to me. We revolted against the accepted canons, values and taste.

Rodchenko met Vladimir Tatlin at Alexander Vesnin's at the end of January or the beginning of February 1916. In his paper on Tatlin, Rodchenko gave an account of this meeting:

I told him how I had tried to participate in the *Mir Iskusstva* exhibition without avail. He also complained, saying, 'I am turning grey and they still refuse to recognize my work! . . . But never mind! Soon we shall stage a Futurist exhibition. Give me your address, and you shall take part in it.'

Some time later V. E. Tatlin came to see me. He looked at my work and said that they had organized a group of exhibitors with himself, L. Popova, N. Udaltsova, A. Exter, I. Pestel, I. Kliun, L. Bruni, K. Malevich and, as a result of our conversation, me, as members. The necessary funds had already been pooled by the exhibitors but since he presumed that I had none, I would have to work for my share, just as he himself was doing. He said he was the organizer and director of the exhibition and I would have to assist him and also sell the tickets, and asked me if this would be all right.

Naturally Rodchenko accepted. The exhibition was soon mounted in an abandoned store on the Petrovka. In addition to the artists already mentioned, Vassileva, Morgunov, Tolstaya and Yustitsky also contributed some works. Both abstract and Cubo-Futurist works were exhibited. Tatlin contributed two *Painted Reliefs* of 1913–14 and two *Counter Reliefs* of 1914–15. Bruni exhibited two three-dimensional reliefs in addition to a broken cement barrel and a bullet-shot pane of glass. Liubov Popova contributed four Cubist compositions. The material presented by Malevich was limited to some Cubist compositions of 1914 and Pseudo-Cubist or 'Alogist' compositions of 1913, among them *An Englishman in Moscow* and *The Cow and the Fiddle*. The latter were listed in the catalogue under the heading 'Alogism of forms'. Rodchenko, who performed the duties of caretaker and ticket clerk, felt richly compensated by the exhibition of ten of his pictures. He exhibited an oil painting entitled *Two Figures* with a pencil study for the same picture, a large composition in oil entitled *The Dancer*, six of his abstract compositions drawn with compass and ruler, and a still-life. The latter was probably either applied or collage work, though the catalogue refers to it as 'tapestry'. All these works had been produced by the artist in 1915.

Cubo-Futurism

After the memorable Futurist evening in Kazan Rodchenko extended his experiments to the fields of both Futurism and Cubism. Among these works the Cubist series of costume designs for one of Oscar Wilde's plays,

The Duchess of Padua [149–50], excels in its bold and consistent style. A change in his repertoire of subject matter also became apparent as the earlier restaurants and carnivals were replaced by new subjects such as sportsmen and the city. Nevertheless, his Cubism and Futurism during the Kazan period remained on the moderate side; Rodchenko's talent and enthusiasm were not in themselves sufficient to master the intricacies of Futurism and Cubism. It would have been logical if on his moving in 1915 to Moscow, the centre of Russian Cubo-Futurism, this situation had changed. This was not, however, the case. In his article on Tatlin, Rodchenko made an interesting admission: while acting as caretaker at 'The Store' exhibition he was also obliged to lead the visitors around and explain to them the essence of the works on show. He did not feel very happy about this; 'I kept explaining the works without understanding Cubism very well myself.'

By the time Rodchenko arrived in Moscow Cubism, Futurism and even Cubo-Futurism, a Russian synthesis of the two movements, were old trends. The latest artistic innovations were represented by Tatlin's experiments with 'real materials' (*Counter-Reliefs*), leading to Constructivism, and Malevich's version of geometrical abstraction, called Suprematism. In their non-objective works, Popova, Rozanova, Kliun, Puni, Udaltsova and others were dealing with colour, a key problem in Russian painting. This was probably one of the most important reasons why Rodchenko showed a comparatively restrained interest in Cubism and Futurism while in Moscow.

The most interesting of his works inspired by these trends is a remarkable preliminary drawing [11] for a picture entitled *Two Figures.* In it the artist unites the figures and the space in an interesting manner, blending forms into each other. It is laconic, accurate but not dry. The harmony between the sharp silhouettes and the inner shading of each form is just as perfect as the harmony among the forms of the composition as a whole. It is Rodchenko's most consistent Cubist work, yet it can only be considered stylized Cubism. In it the role of each form acquires an independent aesthetic meaning. Rodchenko, with his keen sense for stylization, shifted from analysing the structure of objects to revealing the stylistic potential of distortion. The other picture he presented at 'The Store' exhibition, *The Dancer*, evokes so little objective association that we have to consider it as an abstract rather than a Cubo-Futuristic composition.

Neo-Objectivism

Fortuitous circumstances prevented Rodchenko from remaining within the Cubo-Futurist mode. His unique series of twelve abstract drawings executed with compass and ruler at the beginning of 1915, at Kazan, was sufficient to take him directly into the world of truly modern art. The radicalism and conceptual originality of these works – six were shown at

'The Store' – did not only arouse Tatlin's interest: Kasimir Malevich was also greatly impressed, and tried to attract Rodchenko to his side.

Rodchenko's compass-and-ruler drawings already bear the most important characteristics of the version of abstraction that he was to develop during the next couple of years. The term Neo-Objectivism, used in the literature, seems the most appropriate for this work. Unlike Malevich's Suprematism or Mondrian's Neo-Plasticism, Rodchenko's abstraction had no actual programme. The aesthetic justification of Neo-Objectivist compositions is the works themselves. There is no need for supplementary theories or for associations with the complicated world of emotional-psychical phenomena, as in Kandinsky's abstract art. Rodchenko's art might be characterized as consistent formalism or purism.

His thorough knowledge of the characteristics of different materials, and his paramount sense of style, are fully evident in the compass-and-ruler drawings. To paraphrase the title of N. Goncharova's series *The Artistic Possibilities of a Peacock*, one might call Rodchenko's drawings *The Artistic Possibilities of a Compass and Ruler*. By fully exploiting these seemingly inartistic tools, Rodchenko revealed the richness of his fantasy and ingenuity, and when devising the motifs he relied as much on improvisation as on exact calculation [12–15].

Rodchenko's fine intuition preserved him from the twin pitfalls presented by the nature of his means: mediocre ornamentalism on the one hand and aesthetically impoverished pattern-making on the other. In order to avoid ornamentalism Rodchenko deliberately reduced symmetry to a minimum in all his drawings: the composition has no axis, and if it is centralized around one point the centre is usually as far as possible from the geometric centre of the space occupied by the drawing. The two-dimensional figures created by interlocking circles, or circles and straight lines, are never repeated. The individuality of these figures is also emphasized by colour in some of the compositions. It is interesting that most of the forms begin and end beyond the borders of the drawing, implying that they are not chance, isolated formations, but part of a planar universe outside the boundaries of the pictures.

The aesthetic effect of the compass-and-ruler drawings derives primarily from the wide use of contrasts: the play of black and white, the contrast of vivid tones in the coloured works, the interplay of straight lines and curves and of cornered and flexible forms, and finally the contrast of large and small elements, this last particularly enhancing the dynamism of the pictures. Furthermore, in the drawings in which white and black have the same form-creating function, Rodchenko makes extremely interesting and original use of positive-negative effects [12].

Some of Rodchenko's works from 1915 evince an awareness of Kandinsky's expressionistic abstraction [17]. But Rodchenko's amorphous lines and patches, his forays into the world of expressive colour-dynamism, were short-lived and left no lasting effects on his art. His rational and analytical bent, his tendency to feel and recognize only the beauty of clearly readable structures strictly arranged down to the last element, was too strong for that.

Following 'The Store' exhibition, Rodchenko's skill developed rapidly. In the next two years he created a series of wonderful Neo-Objective pictures (in tempera) which are without doubt among the classics of abstract art [19–23]. Only an artist skilful in the use of formal and technical means, who could aspire to and solve the artistic realization of complicated structures brought to life by imagination and will, could have created aesthetic objects so noble in colour and silhouette, so accurate in drawing and proportion and so rich in forms.

In addition to curves, Rodchenko now began to apply increasingly complicated lines. And a true sign of his mature knowledge of colour is his consistent use of its multiple functions: as decoration, as a physical characteristic of an object, and, finally, as paint; that is, as a special material with rich potentials for the development of such qualities as surface texture. As before, Rodchenko continued to use contrasting elements. In addition to those mentioned in connection with his compass-and-ruler drawings, such as colour, angled and flexible forms, etc., in his new series Rodchenko made use of the mutual reinforcement of two- and three-dimensional forms.

Especially original and fascinating in some of the compositions are the finely drawn crystal-like patterns, the outlines of which reflect the colours of the rest of the drawing [22]. This crystal-like character gives tension and meaning to the life of the 'objects'.

Here we need to distinguish between Rodchenko's Neo-Objectivism on the one hand, and Suprematism and Neo-Plasticism, on the other. The impersonal character of the latter two trends of geometric abstraction is alien to Neo-Objectivism, in which certain traditional elements are prominent: the individuality of the act of creation, the role of temperament and taste, the absolute character of the aesthetic value of the work of art, and so on. Thus although it is true that Neo-Objectivism is part of the geometric-abstract trend, it can be classified as such only with serious reservations.

The meaning and content of Neo-Objective compositions are not restricted to decorative values, to beautiful combinations of colours, lines and forms. Almost all of Rodchenko's painted and drawn objects look like the plans for an architectural construction of unknown purpose.

In the creation of his 1916–18 Neo-Objectivist series, Alexander Rodchenko called on all the experiences and knowledge he had accumulated in the preceding years. The continuity between the new series and the compass-and-ruler drawings is indisputable, as is the fertile effect of Cubo-Futurism. Although Rodchenko was certainly not drawn to Tatlin's *Painted-Reliefs* or *Counter-Reliefs*, the influence of Tatlin's creative principles can be clearly traced in Rodchenko's works between 1916 and 1918. Indeed, at one point the abstract 'Engineerism' of Tatlin's *Counter-Reliefs* finds common ground with Neo-Objectivism: both are deeply involved not only with the constructive but also with the inherent aesthetic qualities, such as colour, surface and texture, of metal, glass, wood and other materials. Tatlin played an especially important role in the strengthening of the rational-analytic side of Rodchenko's talent and outlook, bringing out the constructor in him.

1 *In the Restaurant* 1910

2 *Noon* 1910
3 *In the Restaurant* 1913

5 *In the Café* 1912   6 *Portrait of N. A. Rusakov* 1912

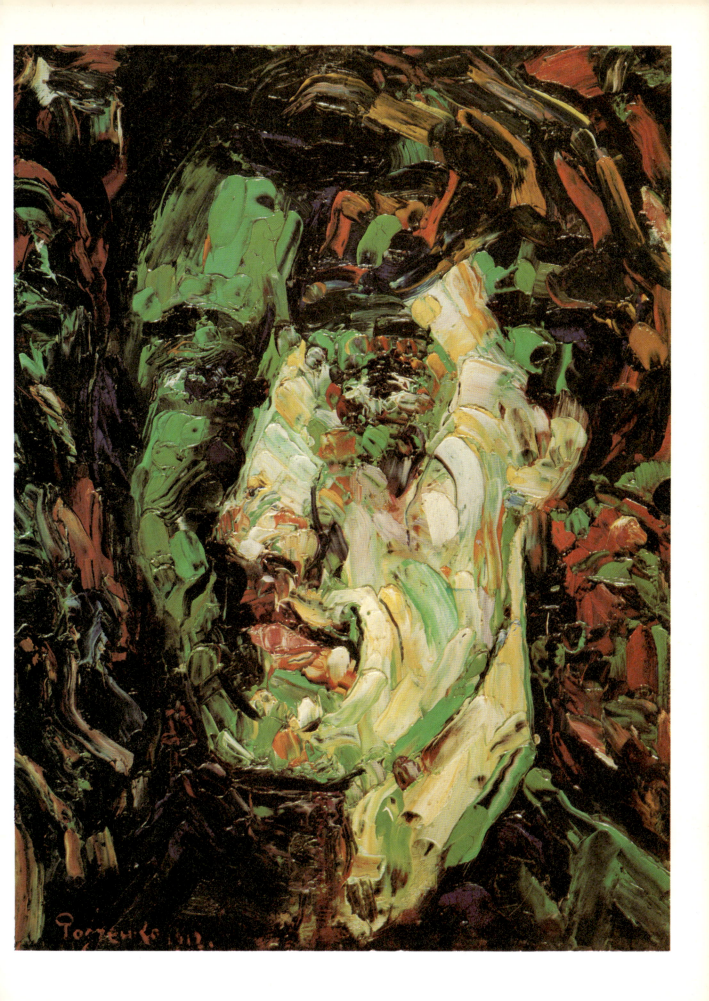

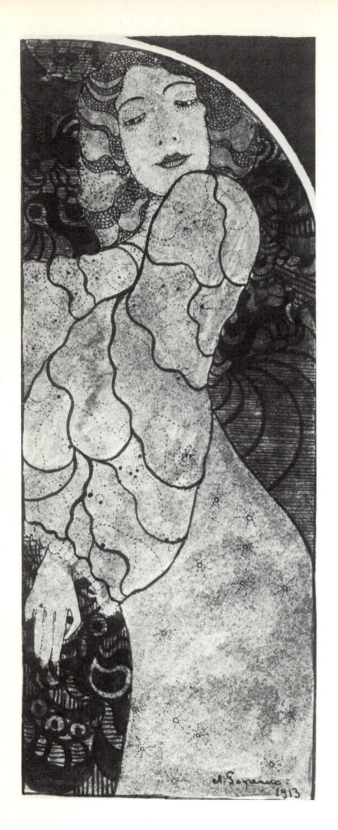 

7 *Woman* 1913
8 *Woman in Kimono* 1913

22

9 *Label* 1913
10 *Landscape in Oriental Style* 1914

11 *Two Figures* 1915

Finally, the influence of Suprematism cannot be overlooked. But it should be emphasized that in this period it was minimal, contrary to some opinions which see Rodchenko as a follower of Malevich.[13] He was certainly not one of Malevich's followers, although he did go through a Suprematist period in his art in 1918 and at the beginning of 1919.

Suprematism

Suprematism emerged as a trend in 1913–14. The first public show of Suprematist art took place in St Petersburg (now known as Petrograd) in December 1915, under the title 'The Last Futurist exhibition, 0.10'. Tatlin's censorious remarks on Malevich's squares, and the conflict they gave rise to, are well known from the literature,[14] although the authors concerned say only that differences existed between the two painters, without actually analysing these differences. A thorough analysis of this complicated and interesting problem goes beyond the scope of this book. It should be pointed out, however, that a valid and detailed evaluation of the conflict is impossible without an extensive and objective analysis of the historical, social and aesthetic roots and the basic tendencies of Russian avant-garde art. It may be added that the deepening differences between Tatlin and Malevich at the end of 1915 had a great deal in common with the conflict that had existed between Larionov and Kandinsky three or four years earlier.[15].

But let us revert to Rodchenko. Everything seems to suggest that until 1916 Rodchenko either knew nothing about Suprematism at all, or had only heard of it. He first met Malevich at 'The Store' exhibition. He recalled this meeting in the following words:

Best of all I liked Malevich's Alogist and Cubist works, apart from Tatlin's, of course. They were fresh and did not remind me of Picasso. But I didn't care for Malevich himself ... he came up to me and said, 'You are the only one here ... but do you know what you are doing?' I said I didn't. Then Malevich said, 'Everything they are doing is old-fashioned and unoriginal. That's past. It is our turn now — the turn of Russian art. That's what I am doing. Come and see me. You have just the right intuition. You are living in the atmosphere of the age!' And he gave me his address.

Rodchenko discussed the matter with Tatlin, whom he had recently found as a friend and supporter, but Tatlin advised him against visiting Malevich.

Not all the works exhibited in 'The Store', the shop on Petrovka, were 'old-fashioned' or 'unoriginal', of course. But Malevich's disparaging words are understandable in light of the December conflict and its immediate results: in deference to an ultimatum issued by Tatlin, who organized the exhibition, Malevich himself had had to rest content with exhibiting his 'old' works rather than his Suprematist ones. The ultimatum obviously did not apply only to him, as there was not one work in the exhibition that showed signs of Suprematism. Little of the material was new to any of the exhibiting artists as they all, apart from Rodchenko and young Yustitsky, knew each other's work well, if only from previous exhibitions. In such a context Rodchenko's radical compass-and-ruler drawings must have given a great impression of freshness. As far as the public was concerned, of course, the whole exhibition contained a great deal that was new and surprising.

So Rodchenko's confrontation with Suprematism could not have happened before the spring of 1916. Furthermore, Rodchenko was shielded from Suprematism for a while by his friendship with Tatlin. Rodchenko's interest in Suprematism, aroused early in 1918, was probably connected with an important event related to the 1917 revolutionary changes. This was the foundation of the Painters' Trade Union, which united all the artists of the radical wing of new art. Although it was a short-lived institution it played a significant historical role, and its advent and brief appearance deserve recording.

In February 1917, with the collapse of the House of the Romanovs, the country attained her long-awaited political freedom. The Czarist Academy of Arts, an institution of evil memory which had governed artistic life in Russia for two centuries, closed on 23 February. At the rallies, meetings and debates of the artist-intellectuals in Petrograd and Moscow a fierce struggle began around the most exciting questions: the culture of the future, the character of the new central institutions, the forms of the associations and the reform of the schools of art.

Regarding the character of the institution which was to function in the place of the former Academy of Arts, two main stands developed shortly. In a manifesto issued in the periodical *Day* (*Den*) on 12 March, 'Freedom of the Arts, an organization uniting artistic, musical and poetic societies, publishers, reviews and newspapers' declared:

Realizing that questions connected with the normal and lawful conditions of artistic life in Russia can only be decided by a *statutory meeting held with the participation of all artists concerned*, and that such a meeting can only be convoked after the end of the war, the 'Freedom of the Arts' association definitely protests against every anti-democratic attempt on the part of certain groups to seize control of artistic activities through the formation of a Department of Arts. The association, therefore, calls upon those in agreement with the present manifesto to appear at the artistic assembly to be held at the Mikhailovsky Theatre at two o'clock today, and to vote for the following persons defending the freedom of art.

The fact that the list of names figuring in the appeal includes that of Mayakovsky clearly indicates which of the two alternatives was the more acceptable to the Futurists. The most active advocate of the proposed Department of Arts was Alexander Benois, evidently supported by many other Miriskusstniks (members of the World of Art circle).

The Miriskusstniks, with Benois at their head, had every hope of filling the leading positions in the new Department of Arts. The strengthening of their power after the February revolution is shown by the fact that in the Special Council dealing with matters of art under the leadership of Gorky, fine arts were represented by Benois, Roerich, Dobuzhinsky, Bilibin, Lansere and Petrov-Vodkin; that is by artists who formed the kernel of the *Mir Iskusstva* group. The monopolistic position of the Miriskusstniks did not bode well for the Futurists.[16]

Nevertheless, the continuation of the war and the internal problems of the country made it essential for the artists and their groups, all enthusiastic partisans of the February revolution, to try to reach at least a temporary agreement. In the summer of 1917, as a result of an interim compromise, the Painters' Trade Union was formed with centres in Petrograd and Moscow. The groups representing different trends had equal rights within the organization.

The Trade Union consisted of three federations: Senior, Central and Junior groups. The Senior, known simple as the Right wing, consisted of the Peredvizhniks; the Centre contained the Miriskusstniks, the Union of Russian Artists, and the Knave of Diamonds; the Junior or 'Left-wing' Federation united the Cubo-Futurists, Suprematists and Non-Objectivists; that is, the radical wing of modern Russian art.[17] For these artists, the Trade Union meant the end of a boycott by society that had lasted for several years. Tatlin was elected president of the Left-wing federation, with Rodchenko as secretary. Rodchenko was also a member of the executive council of the Trade Union Council of Moscow Painters.

The first exhibition of the Painters' Trade Union was held in Moscow in May 1918, not long after the October Socialist Revolution. After slight alterations in the structure of the Trade Union, the second exhibition opened at the beginning of 1919 in the Museum of Fine Arts. Its official title was 'Fifth State Exhibition organized by the Commissariat for Public Education (From Impressionism to Non-Objectivism)'. According to Rodchenko, the Left-wing painters removed their works in protest after the opening, and exhibited them at the Left-wing Federation's club that had opened shortly before. The club consisted of twenty-one artists including Tatlin, Rodchenko, Vesnin, Popova, Drevin, Udaltsova, Exter and Morgunov. It was in this same club that Rodchenko had the only one-man show to be held in his life-time, arousing great interest among the intellectuals sympathetic to modern art.

Finally, in March 1919, the Moscow Painters' Trade Union was transformed into the Federal Union of New Trend Painters with Rodchenko, as well as Kuznetsov, Lentulov, Kandinsky and Udaltsova, on the executive council.

So, at the Revolution, under new circumstances, the radical artists organized themselves, if only for a short time. For a while the antagonism of the previous years partially disappeared and the platforms of art drew closer to one another.

A relatively large group of artists united under the banner of Suprematism. There were, however, essential differences between *their* Suprematism and the orthodox Suprematism of the early followers of Malevich — Puni, Rozanova, Kliun, Popova and others. Although Suprematism was a catalyst in the final elimination of objective associations from the paintings of the Cubo-Futurists, its ideology was quite alien to them. This refers equally to the early, nihilistic ('black square' and 'zero point') period of Suprematism, when objective, psychological and aesthetic associations were eliminated from the work, and to the later 'colour' and 'white' periods (1915–18).

The ideology of the 'colour' and 'white' phases became a component of the involved and rather vague philosophical theory with which Malevich was engrossed at that time, and which represented an individual critique of empiricism. This theory justified Suprematism's method and practice by saying, in Malevich's words, that

the beginning and reason of everything (life) and the true medium of instinctive cognizance is some sort of 'inner excitement' which is pure, inconceivable, inexplicable and whose existence is never verifiable; the cosmic relations of the phenomena of that excitement can only be represented by experimenting with non-objective, elementary and absolute forms.

In the art of Malevich's followers Suprematism, apart from its catalytic influence, was a factor in the creation of a new style. Unlike their master, these artists were primarily concerned with aesthetic formal means. They were not content for long with simple combinations of two-dimensional geometric shapes. As if trying to compensate for the objects and narrative elements that had been expelled from their canvases, they devoted all their artistic energies to the complex formal problems of art. Colour, in all its artistic and physical aspects, remained the constant concern of the whole group; whereas in Malevich's works, even in his 'colourful period', its main function had been to delimit the planes.

By the beginning of 1919, and in some cases much earlier, the artists who had briefly united as Suprematists were calling themselves Non-Objectivists in order to distinguish themselves from Malevich's Suprematism. This included artists, like Rodchenko, who had joined Suprematism later than the others. (It did not apply, of course, to Malevich's pupils at the Second Free Artists' Studio and at Unovis in Vitebsk.) Even Olga Rozanova, who had been one of Malevich's most faithful followers, went over to Non-Objectivism in her last works. The material in the exhibition of 'Non-Objective Art and Suprematism', held in Moscow in the spring of 1919, made clear the character of this process of 'de-Suprematization'. But before going into details of this event, so outstandingly important in the history of abstract art, let us first analyse some of Rodchenko's Suprematist works.

Like his Suprematist predecessors, Rodchenko began his experiments with the simple combination of two-dimensional geometric forms. Among his sketches from 1918, a comparatively large number consists of stripes, an excellent means of creating both static and dynamic rhythmical structures. These were followed by pictures composed of circles, circles and rings, circles and triangles, and circles and rectangles [25, 29–32]. By varying these simple geometric forms, Rodchenko set out to reveal their organic connections and structural possibilities. Gradually the forms became more complicated; ovals and elongated ovals with a third dimension appeared [35–36]. All of these works reflect a maximum precision in the setting and realization of the given task; the design is always strictly constructive.

12 *Compass Drawing* 1915

13 *Compass and Ruler Drawing* 1915

14 *Compass and Ruler Drawing* 1915

15 *Ruler Drawing* 1915

16 *Composition* 1915

17 *Abstract Composition* 1915   18 *Composition* 1916

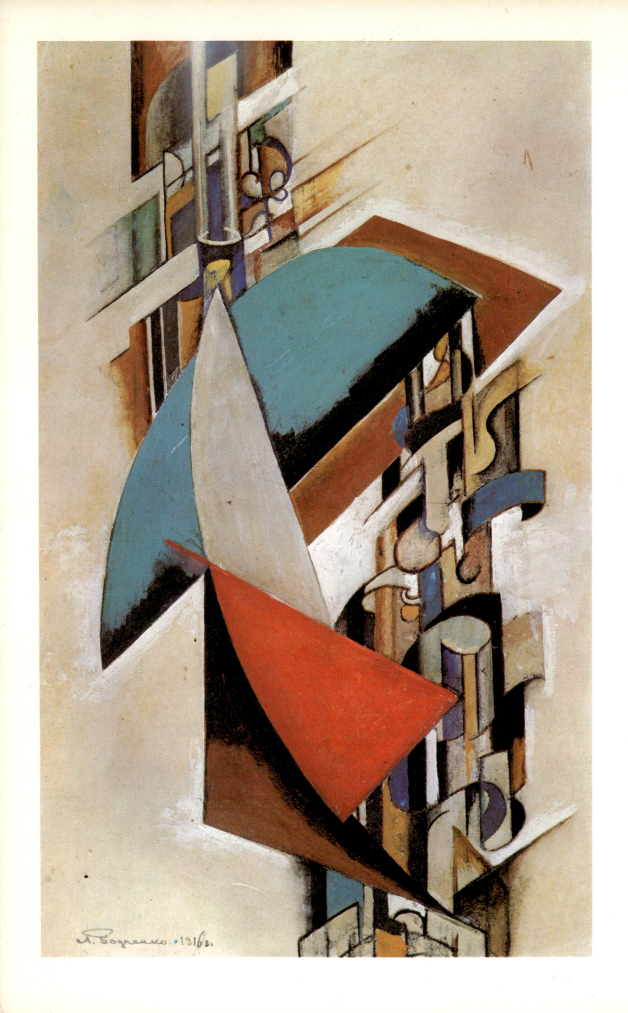

19 *Composition* 1916   20 *Composition* 1917

21 *Composition* 1917

А. РОДЧЕНКО. 1917.

22 *Composition* 1917

23 *Composition* 1918

24 *Composition* 1917
25 *Geometrical Composition* 1918

 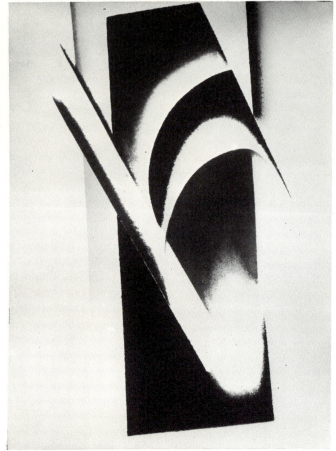

26 *White on Black* 1918
27 *Abstract Painting* 1918

28 *Dancer* 1917

29 *Geometrical Composition* 1918

30 *Geometrical Composition* 1918

31 *Composition* 1918   32 *Composition* 1919

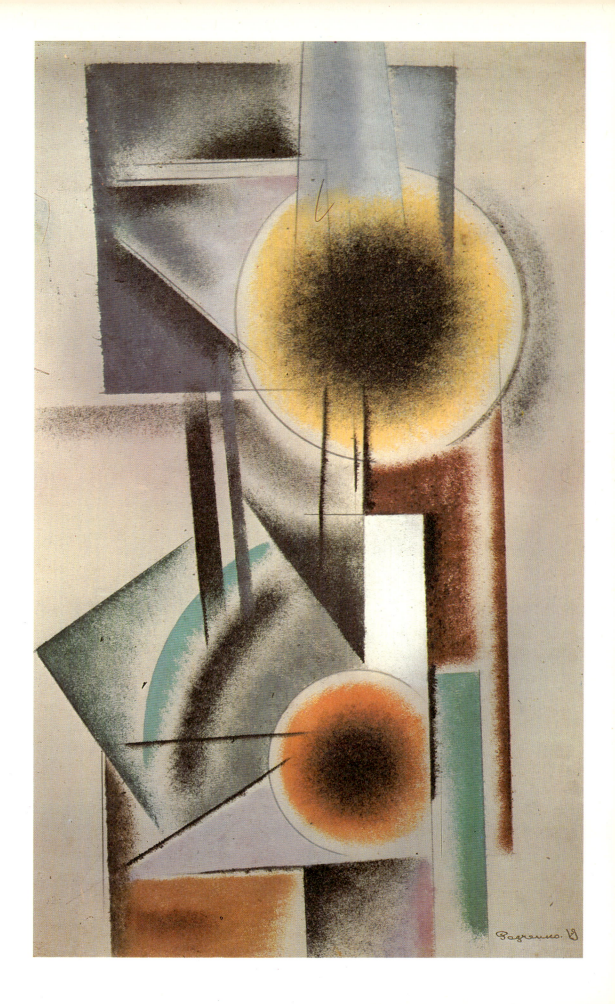

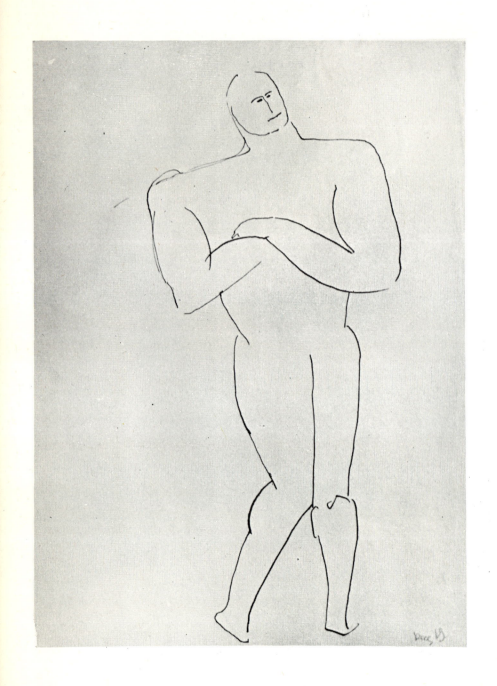

33 *Wrestler* 1919

34 *Wrestler*
1918

35 *Composition* 1919

36 *Composition* 1919

37 *Composition* 1920

38 *Composition* 1920

39 *Composition* 1920

40 *Composition* 1920   41 *Composition* 1920

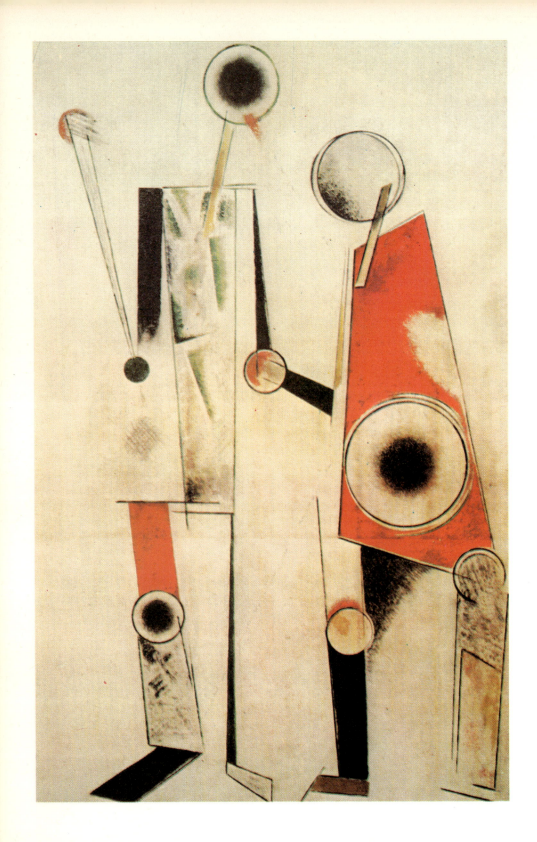

42 *Two Figures* 1919

In the beginning, the colour was also restricted to simple combinations: red and black, blue and black, yellow and black, blue with red and black. As the structures became more complicated, however, the role of colour increased, becoming closely linked with the problems of creating the forms. Colour solidified the structure, while expressing its immanent aesthetic qualities [37–39]. With the widening of the colour range, the role of black also changed. Sometimes Rodchenko used it to subdue and neutralize the colours, and sometimes to bring out the effect of a colour or group of colours by using a black background. It is noteworthy that at the same time Rodchenko started to use mechanical appliances to work the surface of his pictures; instead of a brush, he used roller and stencil.

His series of seven paintings, entitled *Movement of Coloured Planes Projected on Each Other*, and shown at the first exhibition of the Painters' Trade Union in May 1918, is based on an interesting concept and forms a unit complete in itself. Later the same series figured at the Fifth State Exhibition under the title *Complex Compositions of Non-Objective Structure of Coloured Geometrical Planes Projected on Each Other*. The pictures have little connection with Suprematism. In orthodox Suprematist painting geometrical planes are arranged on the canvas in two dimensions; in Rodchenko's pictures the third dimension plays an important constructional role: the flat, oblong figures appear to move in a space which they themselves take an active part in forming. In the catalogue of the first Trade Union exhibition Rodchenko erroneously dated these works as 1916–17; at the second Trade Union exhibition or, to be more accurate, at the 'Fifth State Exhibition', he mentioned only the year 1917. It may be presumed that the series was painted at the end of 1917, and that Rodchenko derived the stimulus for its creation from the experience he had gained through the designs for the Café Pittoresque (see p. 91).

Let us now return to the question of 'de-Suprematization' and to the exhibition staged under the title 'Tenth State Exhibition (Non-Objective Art and Suprematism)' (spring 1919), at which nine contributors exhibited 220 pictures. The catalogue contained the short but emphatic manifestos of seven of the artists. These sought to convince the public of the undeniable historical role and the full artistic value of abstract art. The sympathies and antipathies within Non-Objective art are apparent in these declarations. With the exception of Malevich, all the painters laid a certain degree of emphasis on colour and 'pictorial quality', which they considered the most important factors of an abstract creation. The catalogue began with an article by Varvara Stepanova (under the pseudonym V. Agrarikh) in which she briefly described the character of the graphic works she exhibited:

The new type of Non-Objective poetry, consisting of sound and typography, is combined in my works with painterly sensation, which fills the dead monotonous sounds of the verse with a new, live, visual experience. With the aid of pictorial graphic art I shatter the closely arrayed printed lines, progressing in this way towards a new art. On the other hand, while I am thus recreating the Non-Objective poetry contained in two books, *Zigra ar* and *Rtni khomle*,[18] I introduce sound as a new quality into pictorial graphics, increasing thereby their quantitative potential.

This article is followed by the manifesto entitled 'Non-Objective Art', also written by Stepanova:

Incidentally, I must mention that, in spite of all the lamentations of sworn hostile critics, painting is gaining more and more ground in the world of culture. . . .

If we trace the development of Non-Objectivism in painting, we find two factors of interest. The first – the fight for freedom to create and sanction inventive art as against objective representation – is intellectual. The second is an increase in technical demands. Since Non-Objective painting has discarded the literary from its subject matter, painters have had to raise the quality of their works, – a factor for which their predecessors often substituted the theme of the picture.

Brushwork, skill and technique make high demands, one might even say 'scientific claims' upon the painter; in Non-Objective art it is through these attributes that a picture can attain a high cultural level.

Non-Objective art offers nothing 'obvious' or 'comprehensible', but you should not become indignant over it. You should love art and try to understand the essence of the principle of 'co-existence with art'. It is not sufficient to explore and analyse it, or to delight in its products, expecting only easily understandable scenes and your favourite subjects. . . .

Non-Objective art has not created a doctrinal system and maybe, contrary to previous trends, it never will. On the other hand, it holds thousands of possibilities in store and ensures a wide scope for new developments.

Popova: 'When judged from different aspects, form is not of identical value. The artistic mind has to select the components necessary from the pictorial point of view and filter out the superfluous or artistically worthless ones. . . . The aim of present-day painting is to create "pictorial" rather than "representational" values.'

Rozanova: 'We suggest that art should be freed from the bondage of ready-made forms of reality and turned into a process non-reproductive in character. . . . The aesthetic value of a Non-Objective picture lies in its pictorial content.'

Menkov: 'One should not look at a picture with the preconceived determination to obtain some sort of definitive impression. The coloured surface of the picture will arouse a visual sensation that can hardly be noticed at first. One mustn't expect more.

'As your taste for the coloured surface becomes gradually more refined, you will enjoy the picture more and more.'

In his article, 'Suprematism', Malevich wrote:

Painting was born from a chaotic combination of colours incubated by the warmth of aesthetic power. For the great painters the objects themselves played the role of skeletons only. I find that the nearer we get to painterly culture, the more this framework (formed of objects) loses its own system; it breaks up and gives rise to a different order, an order sanctioned by painting.

The system of Suprematism has conquered the blue of the sky which splintered and dissolved into white in genuine manifestation of the infinite. Thus the sky rid itself of its colour background.

If a picture – even if Non-Objective – has a constructed composition but is based on a mutual relationship between its colours, it will enclose the painter's will within the walls of aesthetic surfaces, instead of opening up philosophical depths. . . .

I have seized the veil of the coloured sky, torn it up, thrown the colours into a sack and knotted it. I have sent them packing to dissolve in the free white depth of infinity.

At this exhibition in 1919 Malevich showed his series called *White on White*. It is not difficult to guess to whom he addressed the words quoted above. They were, of course, meant for the believers in Non-Objectivism, the 'renegades' who had failed to fulfil his expectations. As if in answer to his reproaches, Ivan Kliun, a former Suprematist, wrote these words in his article 'The Art of Colours':

Nature, spattered with paint by the Neo-Realists and Neo-Impressionists, has been broken to pieces by the Futurists. Suprematism has carefully coloured the murdered forms and presents them now as a new art.

Today the art of painting is the corpse of a crudely bespattered Nature; its coffin is sealed with the black squares of Suprematism and exhibited to the public in the new cemetery of art, the Museum of Artistic Culture.

But even if painting as the art of representing Nature has died, its components, colour and paint, are not dead. Released from many centuries of imprisonment by Nature, they have come to an independent life of their own, they prosper freely, and they develop into a new art of colour. Our compositions obey only the laws of colour, not those of Nature. In the art of colour the mass of paint lives and shifts, lending great tension to the colours. The numbed, immobile forms of Suprematism have nothing to do with the new art; all they remind us of is the face of a corpse with a fixed stare.

Malevich had not taken part either in the first or second trade union exhibition; nor does his name figure in the list of the club of the Left-wing Federation. Like other 'Leftist' artists, in 1918–19 he worked for Izo Narkompros (Department of Fine Arts of the People's Commissariat for Education). He taught at the Second State Workshop of Free Artists in Moscow. A large retrospective exhibition of his works ('Sixteenth State Exhibition of Paintings') was staged in the summer of 1919. Yet despite all this Malevich left Moscow in the autumn of the same year and, at the invitation of Yermolayeva, Director of the Vitebsk Peoples' School of Art, he went to Vitebsk. His relationship with his avant-garde colleagues in Moscow had become more and more strained, and this evidently hastened his departure.

At the 1919 'Tenth State Exhibition', entitled 'Non-Objective Art and Suprematism', Rodchenko presented thirty-seven works dating from 1918, which he grouped and characterized as follows:

Non-Objective Art. Works from the first half of 1918. 183–188: Strict static structure, with planes of colour. Simple colour structure. Surface texture. Colour separating from form (this appears for the first time). 189–191: Colours on oval forms. Colours separating from the plane surface create oval shapes, but are not subordinated to them. Motion of colour on oval form. Variety of surface texture and colour on the same surface.

Themes of the second half of 1918. 192–204: Concentration of light colour painting. Freely spreading colour becomes a purpose in itself. Illuminating colour. The light of colour. 205–213: Colour abstraction. Non-illumination (object without colour and light). 214–220: White non-objective statues. Coloured non-objective statues. Plan for Olga Rozanova's memorial.

Next in the catalogue came the description of 'Rodchenko's scheme'. He began his explanation by quoting from men whose ideas were akin to his: from Max Stirner, the fountainhead of anarchism ('As a basis for my work I put nothing'), from the Futurist poet, Alexander Kruchenykh ('Colours drop out, everything is mixed in black'; in contrast to Malevich's *White on White* series, Rodchenko exhibited some *Black on Black* compositions in this show), and from Walt Whitman's *Leaves of Grass*. Then Rodchenko declared his own *ars poetica*:

My rise began with the collapse of isms in painting. At the toll of the funeral bells for colour-painting, we now escort the last ism to eternal rest. The last hopes and love vanish, and I leave the house of dead truth.

It is not synthesis, but invention (analysis) that is the driving force. Painting is the body, creation the soul. My task is to create something new in painting, and my work should be judged accordingly. Literature and philosophy are for the specialists; I am the inventor of new ways in painting.

Stirner's name and aphorism do not appear in the 'scheme' by chance. Like almost every artist and poet of the extreme Left wing of Russian art, on the verge of two revolutions, Rodchenko had been influenced, if none too deeply, by the ideas of anarchism. For lack of further information that would illuminate this episode of Rodchenko's life, it is worth quoting another document which probably dates from the end of 1917:[19]

To the Federal Council of Anarchist Groups.

We artists are compelled to retire from the initiatory group formed under the Moscow Union of Anarchist Groups, because of the intolerable circumstances in which we work.

> V. Tatlin
> A. Morgunov
> A. Rodchenko

To amplify the record of the relationship between Suprematism and Non-Objective Art, here is an interesting document which hints at the complex processes — still not completely clarified — that were taking place in the depths of the Russian avant-garde movement:

> To the Central Museum Bureau.
> *Petition* from Asskranov
> [Association of Extremist Innovators of Painting]

We demand that the former Hludov Showroom be signed over to Asskranov, owing to the sudden death of Suprbez ['Suprematism–Non-Objectivism'], its vitality pouring into the Association of Extremist Innovators of Painting (Asskranov).

15 January 1919

> Rodchenko
> Stepanova
> Drevin
> N. Udaltsova
> A. Vesnin

Beginning of the Constructivist period: Linearism

By 1918 Rodchenko's creative power had fully unfolded. The productivity and variety of styles and forms that characterize the artist's work in the subsequent period is impressive, especially if we take into account the time he devoted to a series of important tasks he undertook as a member of Izo Narkompros.

O. Rozanova and I were engaged in organizing a sub-department of applied arts. We visited workshops, cooperatives and craftsmen, instigating the resumption of work. We restored and granted financial aid to the deserted art schools and supplied them with material.

At the same time Rodchenko took an active part in the foundation of the Museum of Artistic Culture, of which he became the first director. His works were among the most important in the museum. The thirty-seven artists listed in the museum's register included Malevich, Tatlin, Larionov, Goncharova, Popova, Kliun, Rozanova, Lentulov, Filonov, Picasso and Derain.

The majority of Rodchenko's works of 1918 are compositions created under the influence of Suprematism, but a few drawings from his Neo-Objective series of 1916–18, one or two of his Cubo-Futurist pictures, his delicate watercolours of circus scenes [28, 34], and his wonderful abstract lino-cuts showing his reviving interest in line structures [44–46], all date from this time. It was also in 1918 that he created his first three-dimensional structures (displayed at the 'Non-Objective Art and Suprematism' exhibition), and began to take an interest in architecture. Finally, in the same year he started his experiments with lines, giving his endeavours in this field the comprehensive name Linearism.

Rodchenko's enthusiasm for abstract structures, architecture and linear compositions was linked, directly or indirectly, with his activity within a group known as Synthesis of Painting, Sculpture and Architecture (*Zhivopisno-Skulpturno-Arkhitecturny Syntez,* abbreviated Zhivskulptarkh). Among the members of this group, formed at the end of 1918 and the beginning of 1919, were a number of painters (Rodchenko, Shevchenko), sculptors (Korolyev), and architects (Ladovsky, Krinsky and others). We do not know if during the group's three years of existence the members formulated any doctrine of their programme. It is even difficult to determine to what degree, if at all, the activities or even the existence of this group contributed to the development of the Constructivist style which emerged in Soviet architecture and design at the beginning of the 1920s. For Rodchenko himself the 'Synthesis of Painting, Sculpture and Architecture' represented a bridge that led him in the direction of design.

We know of two collective exhibitions of the group, both held in 1920: one entitled 'Zhivskulptura' and the other as part of the Nineteenth State Exhibition, at which the group was allocated a separate room. Rodchenko contributed almost sixty works including twenty-five of his architectural designs.

The beginning and development of Rodchenko's Linearism can be fairly accurately reconstructed. His first line-drawings appeared at the end of 1918, but they were still only sketches, or designs for Non-Objective paintings and abstract sculptural works. A drawing inscribed *Zhiv. Skulpt. Arkh.* [47], exhibiting a boldly drawn spiral structure, occupies an important place among them. On the basis of this and other similar drawings by Rodchenko it may be inferred that the members of Zhivskulptarkh envisaged a synthesis in the literal sense of the word, at least in certain periods of their activity. They did not subordinate painting and sculpture to architecture, but tried to create a new variety of three-dimensional art by blending these different forms of artistic creation. This was in the initial phase of the development of Linearism.

On 22 February 1919 the magazine *Iskusstvo* (*Art*) published Kandinsky's study on 'The Line', and it is almost certain that Rodchenko read it. Our assumption is supported by numerous circumstances, among them the fact that the same issue contained an article by Rodchenko's wife, Stepanova, reviewing Olga Rozanova's posthumous exhibition. In all probability, Kandinsky's study gave Rodchenko further inspiration for his experiments with lines. It is worth quoting a few details from Rodchenko's 1919 workbook:

March–April: I made several dozen Non-Objective pencil drawings in my sketch-book, with and without a ruler.... August: I have decided to paint ten pictures — black on white — with the use of a ruler, on the basis of the drawings I did in April. They will be unusual and novel.... August: Now for the line! May it grow strong through my work.... August: I have started painting pictures of linear themes.... 21 August: I shall surely be strongly criticized for my lines. They will say there is no painting without brushwork. However, I see my task differently. Colour died in the medium of black, and no longer plays a role. Now let brushwork die, too.... 15 October: I have painted my last two linear compositions.

If Kandinsky's lines and Rodchenko's Linearism have anything in common it is probably only the root of the words: in every other respect their compositions differ to the extreme. Kandinsky, whose thinking had remained consistent, regarded the line as a graphic means of expression with unlimited potential, apt to conjure the rarest *frissons* from the depths of the human soul. He stood for the 'world of free drawing' — a world in which 'primitive tools', like the ruler and the compass, have no place. In an article on this subject Kandinsky had this to say:

The line bends, breaks, runs in a variety of directions, and can become transformed. No tool can keep pace with it. We are approaching an age in which a means of expression with infinite potential will reach perfection. The slightest tremor of artistic emotion will obey and be reflected by the fine, flexible line. There are, indeed, playful, bitter, sombre, tragic, frolicsome, obstinate, weak and strong lines, to mention but a few, just as in music, where we distinguish between allegro, grave, serioso, scherzando, etc., according to mood.

Rodchenko's thinking was equally consistent. He was still impervious to the ideas of expressionistic abstraction. He worked with the 'primitive tools' — ruler and compass — and even consciously avoided placing lines of different thicknesses next to each other, lest he should give his composition a 'pictorial' effect.

Rodchenko's Linearism consisted essentially of two formal components whose artistic purposes partly complemented and partly opposed each other. The first, or Neo-Objective component, is represented by the works in which the composition is governed by aesthetic principles. Beginning with simple compositions of straight lines Rodchenko went on to gradually more involved tasks, introducing into his drawings open or closed circular lines as well [48–54]. In his pictures in coloured ink, created in the 1920s, the circle dominates the compositions, while straight lines function as contrasts and preserve their role as an axis designed to keep the construction together. Judging by the surviving drawings and sketches, the painted versions of Neo-Objective linear compositions must have elicited an experience of freshness and surprise.

Naturally the significance of these compositions does not end with the simple aesthetic effect they produce: work with abstract linear structures trains the eye and the hands, and aids in the discovery of the constructive essence of line. Toying with pure linear structures is akin to working with functional ones. Thus the Neo-Objective and Constructivist elements in Rodchenko's Linearism share many traits, in spite of their intrinsic differences.

The artist often created static or dynamic schemes or constructions from linear elements [47, 51, 55]. He executed some of his ideas in material, although only in small dimensions, using mainly panels. He successfully applied the results of his experiments with line to his 'architectural fantasies'; Linearism was also the basis of his radical three-dimensional constructions created in 1920–21 [62–68].

When Malevich asked him in 1916, a propos of the ruler-and-compass series, whether he knew what he was doing, Rodchenko's negative answer was quite sincere. As we have seen, his progress towards abstraction was a logical process, but in those early years his art still contained many instinctive elements. By 1919, he perfectly understood the contents, purpose and significance of his experiments; but by talent and temperament he remained an experimenter rather than a theoretician. Circumstances had not permitted him to acquire a general education in his youth; and later, by the time his intensive self-education bore fruit, the 'cursed art' of easel painting no longer interested either Rodchenko or his fellow-artists. One cannot but regret this: he was an artist endowed with great talent and a keen analytical sense, and on the basis of his practical activity he might have formulated theoretical statements of great interest.

In Rodchenko's notes we read:

I painted my linear pictures in 1919, and they were exhibited in 1920. . . . None of the artists recognized them as paintings at that time, yet by the end of 1920 and the beginning of 1921 imitators of my art were already appearing on the scene. Many said that line as a framework had opened their eyes to the essence of construction.

The lesson drawn from Linearism was summarized by Rodchenko in the short treatise he wrote in May 1921 under the title 'Line':

Line is the first and last factor of painting and of all constructions in general. The line is the path of progress and movement, the point of collision, it is the limit, the link, the section, etc. So line has conquered everything and destroyed the last strongholds of painting: colour, tone, surface texture and geometrical plane.... Putting line in the centre of artistic creation, as the only factor possible to construct with, we simultaneously reject the aesthetics of colour, surface texture and style, for everything that conceals the structure is style (Malevich's square, for example).... Form, colour and surface texture turn into material, and become subordinated to the line, which determines the whole scheme of the construction. Construction in the pure and accurate sense of the word, that is the devising of real objects, can be realized only in material.

Consequently, the effective use of the material is one of the main problems. Construction may be defined as a scheme within which the object is born through the effective use of material. Thus the artist's endeavour to construct has led him through the structural framework to the creation of real objects, that is to say, to the fields of production in general, where he has become the constructor of material systems.

Spatial Constructions

We have seen that in 1918 Rodchenko began to take an interest in material construction in close association with his activity in Zhivskulptarkh. All the activity of the group was related to the art of Tatlin, who in his *Counter-Reliefs* was the first to raise the problem of synthesis. But the artistic and technical issues in which Rodchenko was engaged when he produced his first sculptural-architectural constructions in 1918 had little in common with those solved by Tatlin. Rodchenko was less interested in materials; for him space and form were of primary importance [56–61]. The common features of the 1918 constructions were a support consisting of one or several components, and on this a structure composed of forms that were, as a rule, two-dimensional. These circular, triangular or square elements were built around the axis at varying angles, making a sculpture in the round. The construction had no bulk; instead of closed forms, Rodchenko sometimes used open shapes of two-dimensional curved planes, thus accentuating spatiality and intensifying the effects of light and shadow. The peculiar sculptural and pictorial quality of these planar forms (colour is also sometimes used) provide the aesthetic contents of the works. In technical terms Rodchenko was concerned chiefly with aspects of static and dynamic balance and, of course, with the inherent qualities of the unique structures composed of planar forms.

Other artists produced works similar to Rodchenko's constructions of 1918, but his *Spatial Constructions* of 1920–21 are quite another matter [62–68]. These unique pieces may now be appraised as special representatives and symbols of 'pre-functional' Constructivism. Unlike certain other adherents of early Constructivism, Rodchenko avoided the imitation or stylized rendering of real mechanical or architectural structures; the quasi-technical nature of his works remained hidden and symbolic, while their active function, to proclaim the ideas of Constructivism, was open and dynamic.

43 *Abstract Drawing* 1921

44 *Lino-cut* 1918

45 *Lino-cut* 1918

46 *Lino-cut* 1918

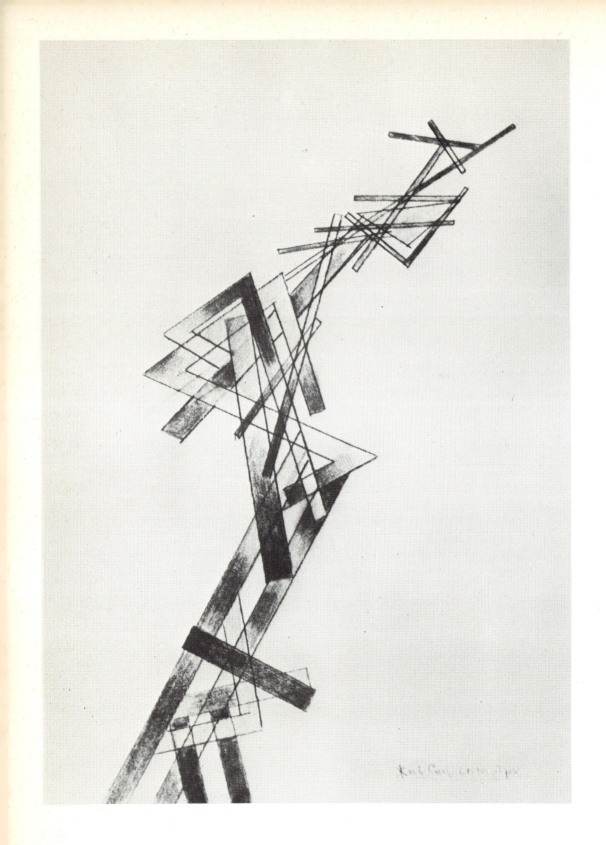

47 *Line Composition* 1918

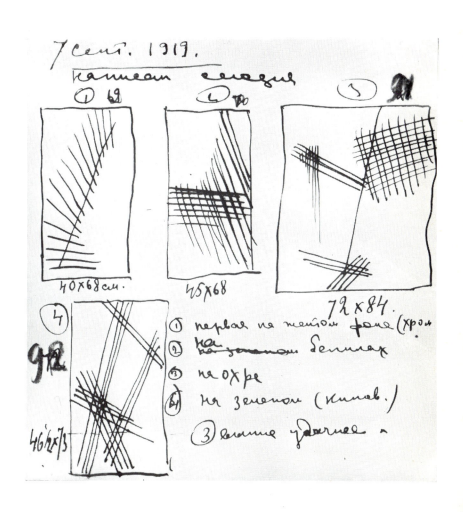

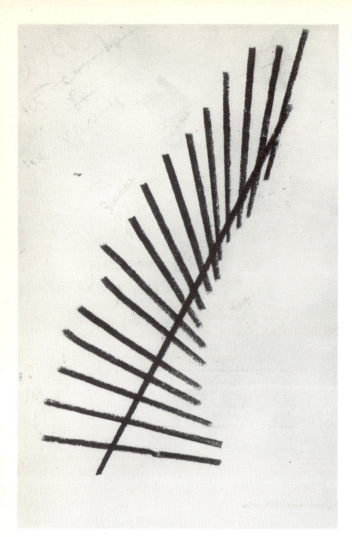

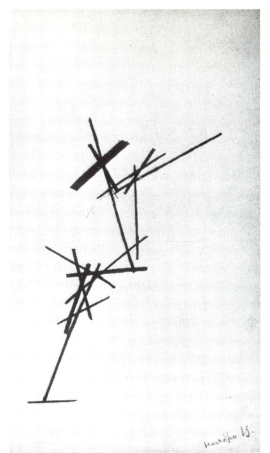

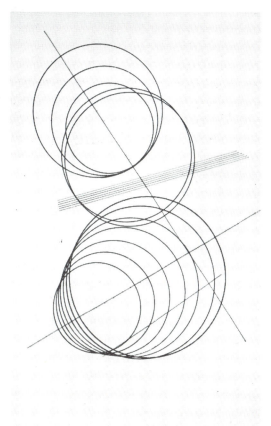

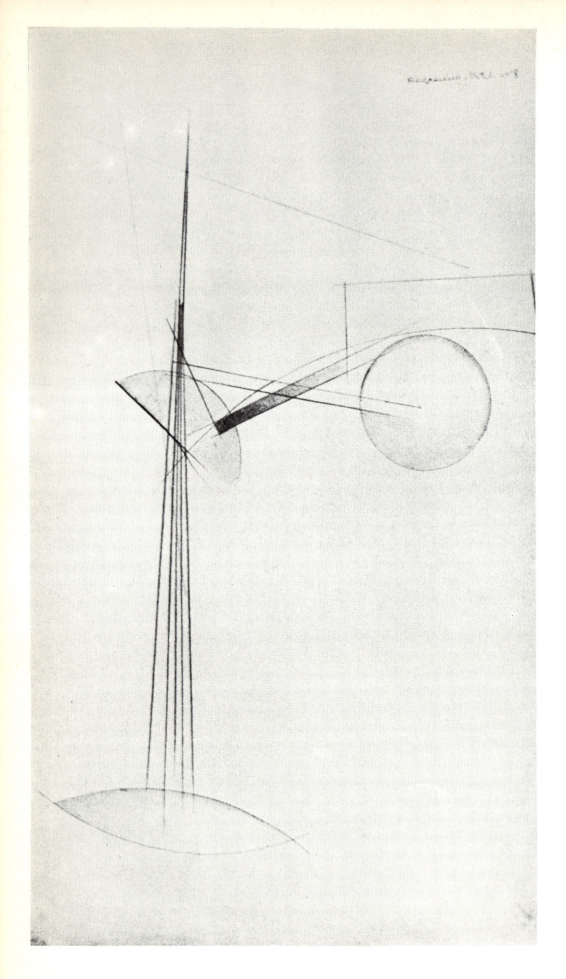

55 *Line Composition*
1921

56 *Construction* 1918

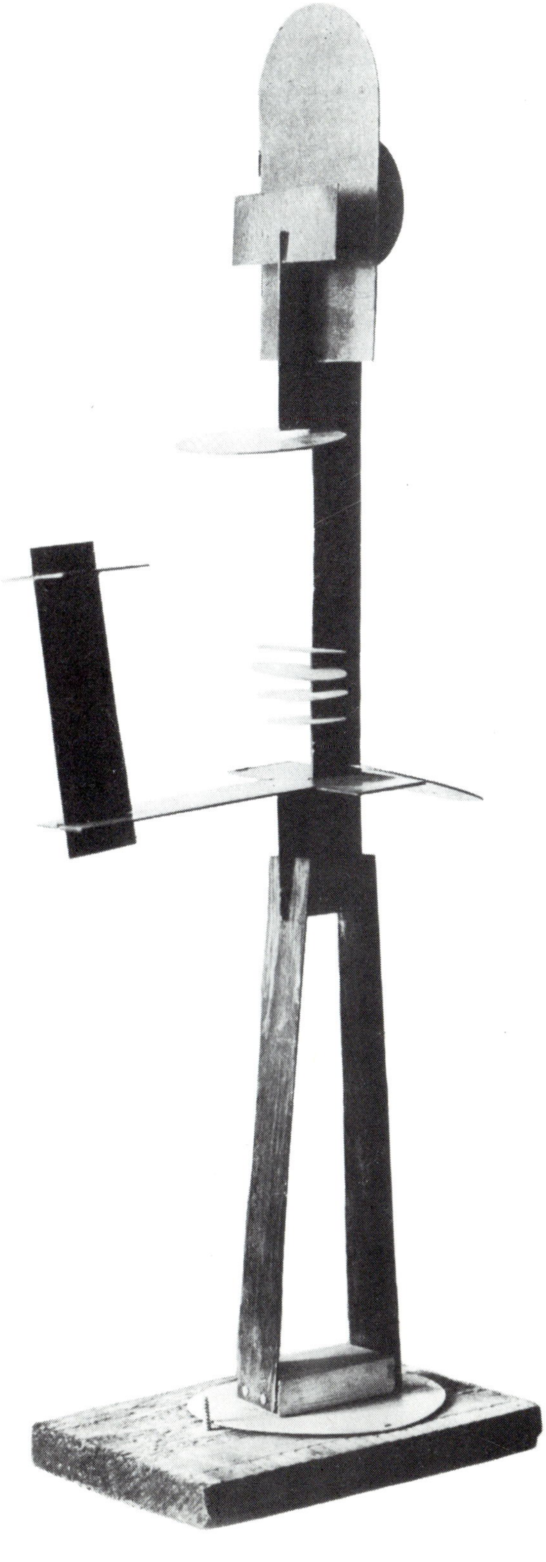

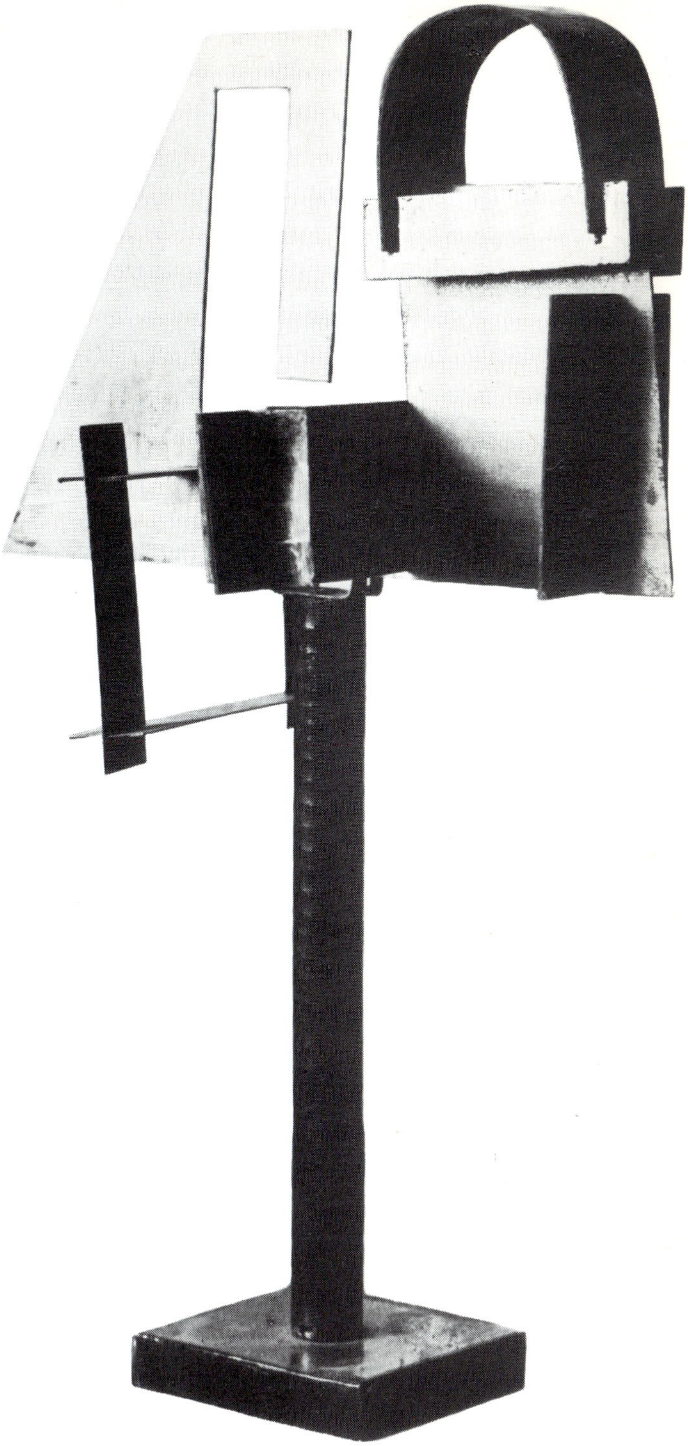

57 *Construction* 1918

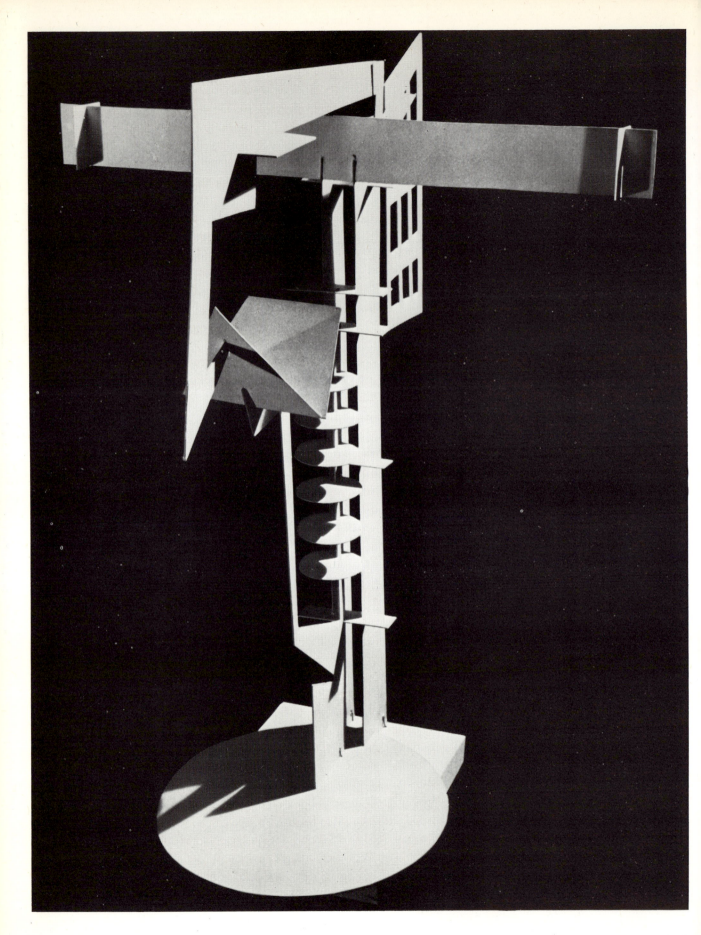

58 *Construction* 1918   59 *Construction* 1918

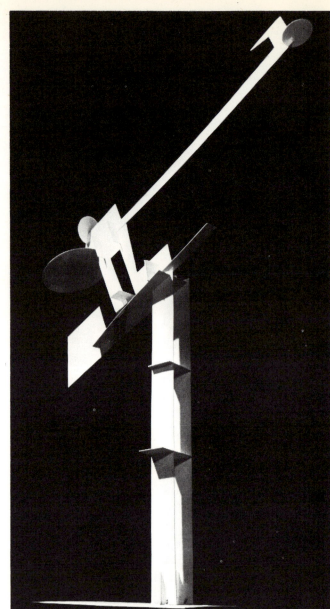

60 *Construction* 1918
61 *Construction* 1918

62 *Spatial Construction* 1920

63 *Spatial Construction* 1920   64 *Spatial Construction* 1920

65 *Hanging Construction* 1920   66 *Hanging Construction* 1920

67 *Hanging
Construction*
1920

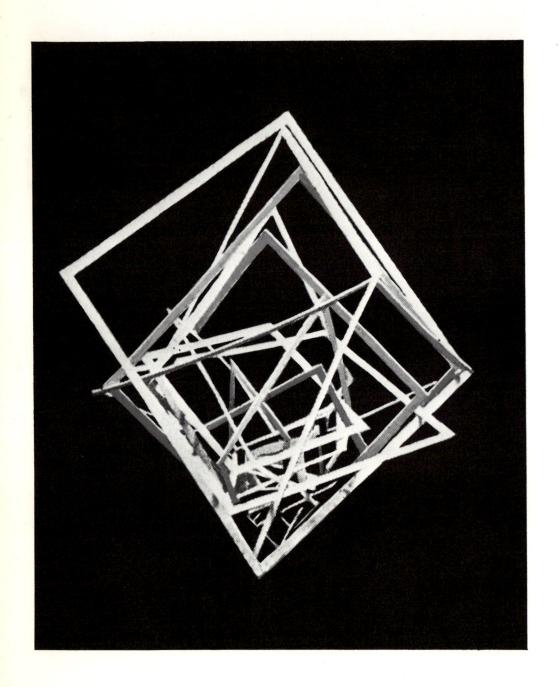

68 *Hanging Construction* 1920

As mentioned before, the foundation of Rodchenko's *Spatial Constructions* of 1920–21 was linear composition. In a sense these later works can also be called linear constructions since each one is built up from straight and curved lines (circles and ellipses). As in linear composition, these spatial constructions were developed from simple to complex forms: from geometrical structures consisting of straight, planar elements to structures of straight and curved lines with more complex spatial relationships.

Nevertheless the linear quality of these constructions is relative. The dimensions of the simple elements which constitute the standing structures [62–64] are important, as they actively contribute to the shaping of space. In the suspended constructions Rodchenko wanted the surfaces of narrow slats placed at various angles to reflect the light falling on them as they rotated [65–68]. In other words, these constructions are an embryonic form of the mobiles which would later occupy the attention of many other Constructivists. Rodchenko built his suspended structures of juxtaposed squares, triangles, hexagons and ellipses of gradually decreasing size, placed on different planes.

One should not be deceived by the small size and plain materials or by the apparent simplicity of Rodchenko's constructions of 1920–21. The criticisms of these characteristics, levelled at his work and that of other artists, were self-evidently unjust even at the time. Rodchenko turned to simple materials for two equally important reasons. The first was a practical one: the World War, the Revolution, and the civil war had caused such devastation and poverty that even the materials he did employ – wood, cardboard and plywood – were considered a luxury (for drawings he was compelled to use wrapping-paper, printed matter, and the backs of illustrations torn from old magazines). The other reason was a subjective one. An obvious trait of his artistic personality was a predilection for serial work. Whenever he hit upon a fascinating problem of form and technique in his experiments, he was quick to discover its potential: proceeding from the simple to the intricate, he would produce ten to twenty different versions before going on to the analysis of the next problem. Constantly driven by a craving for new experience, once Rodchenko had found a satisfactory solution to whatever artistic problem happened to be absorbing him at the moment, he had no desire to exploit it any more. Moreover, the execution of constructions in precious materials – such as metal or glass – is time-consuming and requires special technical skill. Indeed, even if Rodchenko had had adequate financial and technical means, it would probably not have changed his working methods appreciably.

At that time Tatlin and Malevich were often condemned for their 'technical incompetence' and their 'naïve-romantic technical approach'. Their experimental work was criticized for its 'destructiveness'. Today there is no need to defend Tatlin or Malevich against such charges, for their roles in the history of Constructivism have become well known and are indisputable. But for various reasons Rodchenko's role is less widely known today, even though the work he produced between 1917 and 1921, that is in the decisive period of the development of Constructivism, was no less significant than the works of the older artists. The progressiveness and originality of Rodchenko's art was recognized in 1920 when his fame and reputation greatly increased. From this time on he became one of the most active members of the Institute of Artistic Culture in Moscow (*Institut Khudozhestvennoy Kultury*—Inkhuk) and his name figured on the list of teachers active at Vkhutemas (an abbreviation for the Russian name High-Grade Art-Technical Workshops). This was the first time since 1916 that Rodchenko had achieved social and artistic advancement without the support of Tatlin, who was living in Petrograd at that time.

Rodchenko's growing fame was connected with another event which took place in 1920. The artist recalled:

It was on 2 October 1920 that fifty-seven of my works were put on show at the Nineteenth State Exhibition. It was arranged in the Salon in Bolshaya Dmitrovka, and Mayakovsky was also at the opening. He came up to me and said, 'Come along, Lilya Yurevna Brik wants to meet you.' That is how I got to know Mayakovsky.

Identical views and similar work soon turned Rodchenko's and Mayakovsky's acquaintance into friendship. The art of Soviet book and advertising design in the 1920s owes a series of epoch-making works to the cooperation of the artist and the poet.

PART TWO

Productive work

In 1921 a small group of 'Leftist' artists, including Rodchenko, broke away from pure art to make direct contact with productive work. The concept of Productivist art (design) was formulated in Russia in the course of prolonged social, technical and cultural development. The October Revolution accelerated this process and emphasized the social aspects of design. A few facts and documents will permit deeper insight into the events.

From the very first months of its existence the young state evinced a lively interest in the applied arts which, apart from anything else, were regarded as a useful means of restoring the ruined economy. In 1918 the Trade Union of Artist-Painters of the New Art was founded in Petrograd with painters, sculptors and architects as members. The Union conducted five competitions for its members: architectural plans for a building, plans for the interior of a worker's flat, designs for costumes, for a tea-set, and for a knife, fork and spoon.

During the summer of 1918 the Committee of Applied Arts was established. This was a body attached to the Scientific-Technical Department of the Supreme Council of the People's Economy. The task of the Committee was specified in its programme, which said:

The principal aim of the Committee of Applied Arts is to develop and support the artistic creativity of the people. . . . In their spiritual essence, the applied arts are inseparable from architecture, painting and sculpture. They have to solve the same problems except that the products of applied arts are utilized directly in the everyday life of the masses, creating festive, joyful conditions for human existence. . . . There is another important point, notably that by their contribution to increasing exports, applied arts greatly promote the economic rise of the country.

That August the Sub-Section of Applied Arts, headed by Rozanova with Rodchenko as her deputy, was established within Izo Narkompros. The work of organizing workshops for training industrial artists and of setting up industrial studios equipped with their own laboratories was one of the duties of the Sub-Section. At the beginning of 1919 this institution was converted into the Applied Arts Committee of Izo, representing artists, experts, and their union. The Committee dealt with all questions, from those concerning the training of craftsmen in applied arts, to those concerning the organization of industrial art production. It exercised full control over the aesthetic aspects of design in the manufacturing industry.

In May of 1919 the department designed to deal with artistic work proposed that artists form creative collectives. Within a year the organization registered eleven groups (including Zhivskulptarkh and Obmokhu, the Society of Young Artists),[20] and arranged a number of competitions (the design of a newspaper kiosk, posters for the anniversary of the October Revolution, etc.). The first All-Russia Conference on issues of the applied arts, organized by the Applied Arts Committee, was held in August 1919 and the same year saw three exhibitions of applied arts.

Obviously the young state was interested in developing the applied arts, and it supported work in this field as far as circumstances permitted. The form of this development, however, depended on the artists and specialists.

In 1919 the first sporadic attacks were launched against traditional decorative art in the name of modern industrial design and its principles. It was the critic and art historian Nikolai Punin who had first formulated the ideological motives and the theoretical concepts of future Productivist art in his address on art at a meeting held in the Palace of Artists (the Winter Palace) on 24 November 1918. The subject of the meeting was 'A sanctuary or a factory?' The speeches of the participants were published on 17 December 1918 in the journal *Iskusstvo Kommuni* (*Art of the Commune*). In view of the importance of the thoughts expounded by Punin, nearly the whole text of his address is quoted here.

The bourgeoisie conceived of art as something sacred with artists as its priests. The bourgeoisie regarded art as a sanctuary to be entered only trembling and in fear. Owing to the bourgeosie, creative artistic activity became a sort of devout rite.

The proletariat cannot have such an idea of art. The hungry masses were not given the privilege of meditating calmly in the world of art. And this is just as well, since they have preserved their direct, pure comprehension and appreciation of art. At present it is too early to speak about proletarian art. For the moment there is no such thing. But there will be, there must be. Proletarian art will be unlike bourgeois art. The proletariat which has overthrown everything will also have to create a new art. There is no proletarian art yet, but the path which leads to it can already be seen. The proletariat is a powerful creative force producing day after day things of genuine value. *It knows exactly what material is. For instance, no artist knows surfaces as well as certain skilled workers do. The proletariat extends an artistic conception to our everyday life and environment. Bourgeois artists only designed ornamental pieces, leaving their realization to the craftsmen. The latter produce the objects themselves. They have a flair for seeing their inherent qualities. An entirely new era in art is sure to follow. The proletariat will create new houses, new streets, new objects of everyday life.*

Two points should be noted about Punin's address: one is that he was the first to define and distinguish decorative art and 'productive' art. The other is that, by emphasizing the object, Punin became one of the precursors of the philosophy of Veshchism (Objectism). He continued:

We need plain utilitarian objects of good quality and artistic execution. Those who want and are able to work for the new state should go to furniture, textile, and china factories, timber yards and so on, and should think about the requirements and tastes of the proletariat, endeavour to satisfy these requirements and tastes, since that is all that is needed.

In 1920 and 1921 the ideology of Productivist art was established by Inkhuk in Moscow. This institute, founded in May 1920, aimed 'to develop a science dealing with the various branches of art and investigating the basic question of art as a whole' (from the statutes of the

Institute). Kandinsky took a very active part in setting up Inkhuk in Moscow. Tatlin was a corresponding member and later, at the end of 1921, organized its Petrograd group, while Malevich made similar attempts at Vitebsk. The first programme of Inkhuk was developed by Kandinsky in 1920. In many respects the views expounded in it are still valid. A later report by the Institute reflects developments in the activity of the Moscow centre:

Kandinsky collaborated directly in its organization. However, it soon became evident that a profound divergence of views existed between him and the other members of the Institute. Believing in the psychological approach, Kandinsky sharply disagreed with the opinion of those who defended the material 'object' as the substance embodying the value of creative work. He left the group, while Rodchenko, Stepanova, Babichev and Bryusova became members of the administrative board.

Thereafter the Institute continued its activities with the group of Object Analysis, in accordance with a plan and programme worked out by Babichev. Research was performed in two directions:

1. Theoretical: analysis of works of art, definition of fundamental problems of the fine arts (colour, texture, material, construction, etc.). This work was done in direct contact with the products of art involved, mostly in the museums.

2. In the laboratory: the themes treated by the members of the group were individual or collective (for instance, each member wrote a study on composition and construction).

By the spring of 1921 the characteristic conception of this phase in the Institute's activities had taken shape. The single word, 'object', expresses its essence. A late echo of this period was the journal *Veshch, Gegenstand, Objet* [*Object*], founded early in 1922 in Berlin by Lissitzky, a member of the Institute.

From the very moment of its inception, however, this ideology provoked a reaction among the members of the Institute which was directed 'counter the object', 'against pure art'.[21] This anti-object movement became known as Constructivism.

In 1921 the work of Inkhuk rested on a Productivist basis; the immediate consequence was that the 'Leftist' artists who refused to give up easel painting (Kliun, Drevin, Udaltsova and Korolyev) resigned. From this time onwards Tatlin, Rodchenko, Popova, Stepanova, and Vesnin threw in their lot with the new tendency.

Thus Veshchism was the early stage of Constructivism, corresponding to the phase of 'laboratory art'. It attempted to reconcile Productivism with modern tendencies in the fine arts, although one of the important points in the Productivist programme, at least in Russia, was the complete denial of pure art, proclaiming the death of easel painting. In *Veshch*, edited by Lissitzky and Ehrenburg, Veshchism was formulated as follows: 'Every organized product — a house, an epic poem, or a picture — is an object with a rational function.... *Veshch* believes that the poem, the visual form, vision itself, are all functional objects.'

When the Constructivists had advanced beyond the ideology of Veshchism, they continued to stress the term 'object' for a while. The following passage is from Alexei Gan's passionate, rather confused work, *Constructivism*, published in 1922:

This century is the century of technology. So sculpture has to bend to the spatial solution of objects. Painting cannot vie with photography. Theatre becomes ludicrous when one can watch the spectacle of the masses on the move.... Technical implements are not simply external objects but the extended organs of society, social instruments. Hence objects acquire a meaning as elements of social existence, they belong to human society as its technical system which organizes the working process.... The chief error of Comrades Ehrenburg and Lissitzky is that they are unable to break away from art. They simply identify new art with Constructivism.

Our Constructivism is militant and unappeasable : a hard battle is being fought against the gouty and the paralytic, against Right- and Left-wing daubers, in a word against all those who protect, in the slightest measure, the speculative function of art.

In 1920 Mayakovsky joined in the debate. On 19 December 1920, for example, he gave an address on 'The Poetry-processing Industry' at the Polytechnic Museum. His theses were: (1) Artists — a social stratum to be liquidated; (2) Art of Industry? (3) Against all trends. At the close of 1922 and early in 1923 Mayakovsky organized the Lef (*Levii Front Iskusstva* — Left Front of Art) group which united poets, artists, critics and theoreticians on the platform of Productivism, or 'Life-building', to use Nikolai Chuzhak's term.

Rodchenko became one of the central figures of the Productivist movement. In 1920 his art had only reached the stage of 'laboratory experiments', but his dreams soared into 'the constructively organized future', in which the whole of life was to be organized directly by the artist-constructor, the artist-engineer. At the Nineteenth State Exhibition of 1920, where his works were displayed in the room adjacent to Kandinsky's, he stated his Constructivist convictions on a typewritten page pinned to the wall.

Non-objective painting has left the museums; non-objective painting is *the street, the square, the town and the whole world itself.* The art of the *future* will not be a pleasant ornament for family homes. Skyscrapers forty-eight storeys high, enormous bridges, the wireless telegraph, airships, submarines, etc., will all become art.

In February 1921, Rodchenko compiled a collection of slogans related to 'Construction', the subject he taught at Vkhutemas. This collection of slogans contains in a concentrated form the essence of Productivist ideology:

Slogans

Construction is the arrangement of elements.
Construction is the outlook of our age.
Like every science, art is a branch of mathematics.
Construction is the modern prerequisite of organization and the utilitarian employment of material.
Art that is useless for life should be kept in museums of antiquities.
The time has come for art to be an organic part of life.
Constructively organized life is more than the enchanting and stifling art of magicians.
The future is not going to build monasteries for priests, or for the prophets and clowns of art.
Down with art as a glittering extravagance in the senseless lives of the wealthy!
Down with art as a showy gem in the dark, grimy lives of the poor!
Down with art as a means of escape from a senseless life!
The art of our age is conscious, organized life, capable of seeing and creating.
The artist of our age is the man able to organize his life, his work and himself.
One has to work for life, not for palaces, churches, cemeteries and museums.

Active work has to be done among the people, for the people, and with the people; down with monasteries, institutions, studios, studies and islands!
Consciousness, experiment . . . function, construction, technology, mathematics — these are the brothers of the art of our age.

These slogans were not 'Leftist' phrase-making or posturing, but the organic components of the artist's ideology. Their markedly Socialist character is the natural outcome of Rodchenko's earlier hard life and circumstances.

In his study entitled 'Line' (May 1921), Rodchenko gave a detailed interpretation of the slogan 'Down with art as a means of escape from a senseless life':

Not only are we surrounded by decorative, mendacious objects which drive people to take refuge in churches, museums and theatres, but we fail to understand, value, and organize life itself. . . . People are bored, they consider their work dismal, dull and a mere pastime; apart from a few rare exceptions, they regard their lives as monotonous and empty, because they do not appreciate that man himself is able to construct, to build and to ruin.

Utilitarian objects: the end of easel painting

Rodchenko had already worked on utilitarian objects prior to the period of Productivist art. The first real opportunity to test his abilities as a constructor presented itself in 1917, shortly before the October Revolution, when, as a member of the Moscow 'Leftist' group of artists, he took part in the interior decoration of the Café Pittoresque. Rodchenko wrote:

The owner of the café was a capitalist by the name of Filippov. Nearly all the bakeries in Moscow belonged to him. He probably wanted to have a completely original coffee-house. Yakulov was commissioned to decorate it. . . . Yakulov invited me and also Tatlin to share the work.

The designers wanted the Café Pittoresque (known after the October Revolution as the Red Cock Café and subsequently as the Coffee-house of the Revolutionary City) to represent the synthesis of fine arts, literature, and theatre. Yakulov defines its role as follows:

The second half of the nineteenth century changed the urban image, enriching it with the introduction of electric light, new means of communication, and industrial development. All these factors have expanded the emotional sphere of creativity. They lure the artist out into the street, as apartments are cramped and palaces have become obsolete. There is no open sky; it is visible only to peasants. The staple food of twentieth-century urban populations is the city itself, the railway stations and factories. Painting's search for new paths came to an end when, having turned to popular creative forces and style, it discovered its own true nature and found its emotional essence in the theme of the modern city.

The Café Pittoresque set out to evoke the aesthetic problems of the modern city and lay the foundations of the new style both in painting and in the other branches of art.[22]

Tatlin, Rodchenko, Udaltsova, Yakulov, Bruni, Bogoslavskaya, Tolstaya-Dimshits, Golova, Golochapov, Shaposhnikov and Rybnikov all took part in the decoration of the café. It was hoped that the painters Anyenkov, Kuznetsov and Ulianov, the poets Mayakovsky, Kamensky, Khlebnikov and Burliuk, and the theatre director Meyerhold, would join in the life of the establishment later. An eye-witness gave the following account of the remarkable décor of the café:

The interior decoration of the Café Pittoresque astonished young artists by its dynamism. Fancifully shaped objects of cardboard, plywood and cloth — lutes, circles, funnels, spiral constructions — were fitted with electric lights. Everything was flooded with light, everything revolved and vibrated, everything seemed to be in motion. Red and orange dominated, set off by contrasting cold colours. These strange objects hung from the ceiling and sprang from the walls, their boldness astounding whoever saw them.[23]

One group of artists designed the ornamental objects, while the rest, Tatlin, Udaltsova and Bruni, were engaged in executing the plans. Rodchenko decorated the ceiling and designed other decorative elements in addition to nearly twenty of the lamps [69–71].

These first attempts to produce utilitarian objects constituted the first serious test of the modern Russian design movement. Rodchenko's designs manifested several important features of the future designer-artist's work: ingenious and modern conception, inherent unity of the aesthetic nature and the function of objects, and economy. The interplay of forms did not become an aim in itself, but was subordinated to the principal function of lighting. Some of the lamps emitted a narrow, directional beam of light; another type gave a diffuse light. In the design of a third kind Rodchenko strove to produce two or more directed rays of light from the same source and to use thermal currents to make the structure revolve. The ornamental quality of the constructions was enhanced and diversified by colour effects. Rodchenko's lively imagination was equal to the challenge: although he used very plain elements, every lamp was given a unique form. Finally, it is characteristic that though the lamps were planned for a café, they could have been used in other settings, even in a flat.

Rodchenko's fondness for designing 'architectural fantasies' primarily served to stimulate his personal development, but some of his works in this field are noteworthy in their own right. Both in its details and as a rational solution to an architectural problem, Rodchenko's plan for a News Kiosk [72] is especially interesting. The design was submitted for a competition held by the Sub-section of Applied Arts and was awarded the second prize. Before that it had been on show at the Eleventh State Exhibition in 1919 (the number of exhibitors and of items displayed, 176 and 1076 respectively, gives an idea of the size of this exhibition).

Since there were no technical difficulties involved, Rodchenko was able to devote his entire attention to the architectural forms of the kiosk; moreover, he had the opportunity to do justice to his concepts of 'pictorial-sculptural-architectural synthesis'. It would be interesting to trace the relationship of the newspaper kiosk and other architectural designs to the abstract architectural forms Rodchenko had devised in his 1918 structures and Non-Objective drawings and paintings [40–41].

69 *Lamp for the Café Pittoresque* 1917

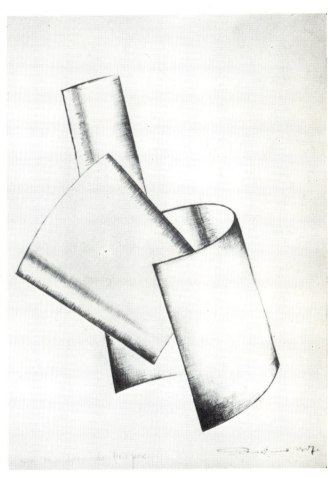

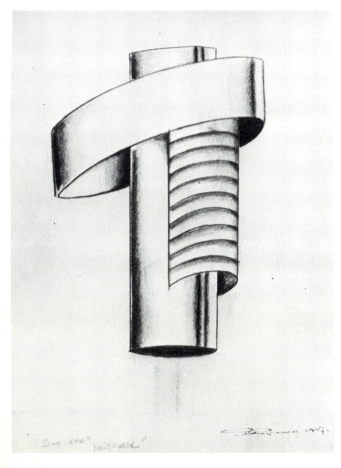

70 *Lamp for the Café Pittoresque* 1917

71 *Lamp for the Café Pittoresque* 1917

72 *News Kiosk* 1919

73 *Airport* 1918
74 *Building* 1920

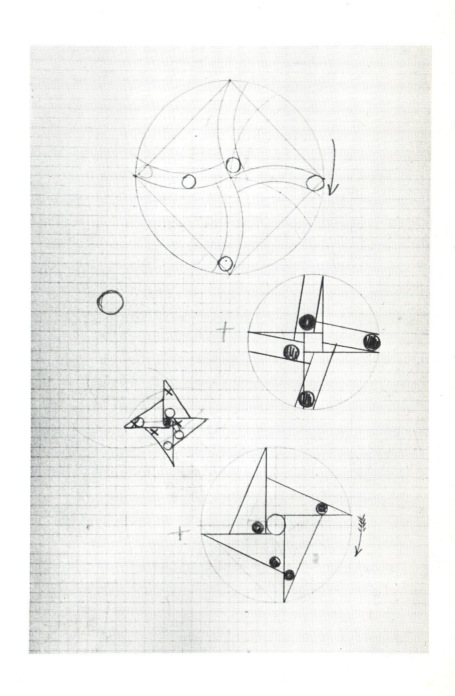

75 *Emblem* 1925
76 *Emblem* 1925
77 *Perpetuum Mobile* 1921

Noqnoe.

78 *Tray* 1922

79 *Teacups and Tray* 1922

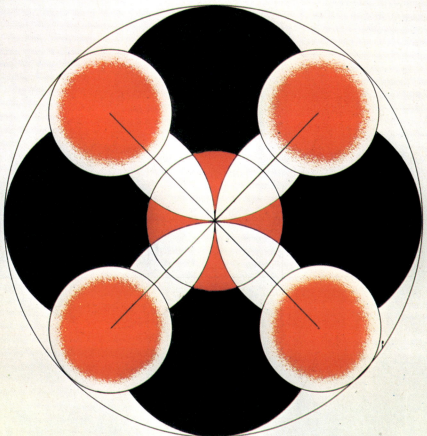

Чашка и блюдце.

Родченко. (эмал. прома.)

81 *Trade Mark for Dobrolyet* 1923

Goodplane.

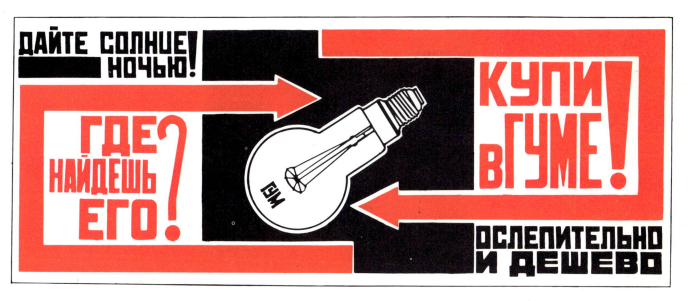

82 *Poster* 1923

Give sunshine at night!
Where will you find it?
Buy at GUM!
Dazzling and cheap.

80 *Advertisement* 1924

All new publications.

83 *Trade Mark for Mosselprom* 1923

Nowhere but Mosselprom!

84 *Poster* 1923

Better teats or dummies
Never were nor are.
Ready to suck till old age comes.
On sale everywhere. Rubbertrust.

ЛУЧШИХ СОСОК

НЕ БЫЛО И НЕТ

ГОТОВ СОСАТЬ ДО СТАРЫХ ЛЕТ

ПРОДАЮТСЯ ВЕЗДЕ

РЕЗИНОТРЕСТ

ХВАТАЙТЕСЬ
ЗА ЭТОТ
СПАСАТЕЛЬНЫЙ
КРУГ!

ГУМ

ВСЕ
ДЛЯ
ВСЕХ

ДОБРОКАЧЕСТВЕННО
ДЕШЕВО!
ИЗ ПЕРВЫХ РУК!

85 *Poster* 1923

Seize on this lifebelt.
Everything for everyone!
Good quality,
Cheap,
Brand new.

86 *Poster* 1923

All that remains of the old world.
Ira cigarettes.
Nowhere but Mosselprom.

87 *Poster* 1923

Stop the traffic!
Remember Mosselprom biscuits are best.
Nowhere but Mosselprom.

88 *Sweet-wrapper* 1923

Our industry. Red October.
In the spring the earth is black,
swollen like cotton wool.
Give larger seed.
Cultivated elevator.

89 *Sweet-wrapper* 1923

Our Industry. Red October.
Don't stand by the river for ever,
It's better to build a bridge.

90 *Poster* 1923

Man needs a clock.
For clocks only Mozer.
Mozer only at GUM.

91 *Poster* 1923

Three Mountain Beer.
Away with home-brew!
Mosselprom.

92 *Poster* 1923

Rubbertrust.
Protector in rain and slush.
Without galoshes, Europe can only sit down and cry.

93 *Poster* 1923

Easterners.
Buy up!
The camel brings
you best galoshes.
Rubbertrust.

94 *Poster* 1923
Dobrolyet.
Shame on you if your name is not
yet on the shareholders' list.
The whole country follows these lists.
Dobrolyet shares will build the aviation industry.

95 *Poster* 1923

There's far to go.
One wall is not enough.
Be ready to change the old men.
Read the journal *Change*!

96 *Advertisement* 1924
Look.

97 *Advertisement* 1924
News.

98 *Advertisement* 1924
News.

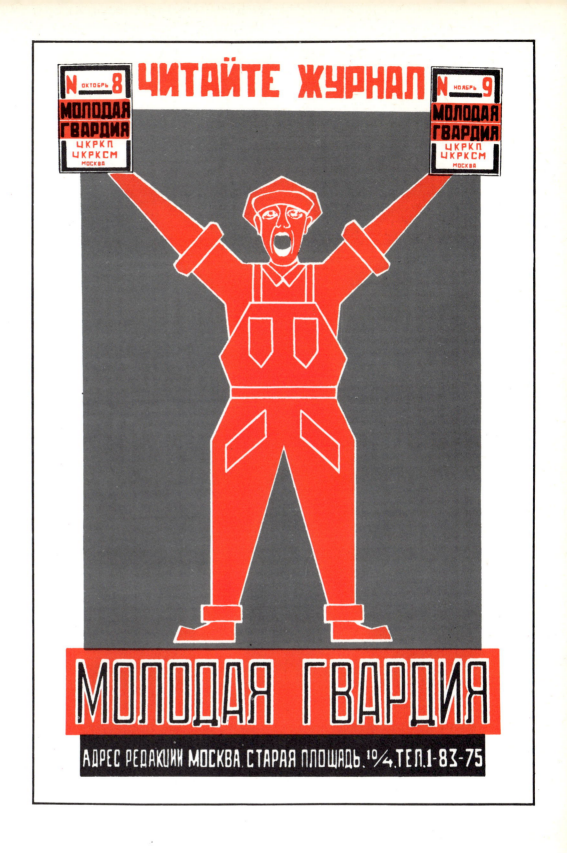

99 *Poster* 1923

Read the journal *Young Guard*.

100 *Advertisement* 1925

Lengiz books in all branches of knowledge.

101   *Trade Mark for Federatsiya Publishers* 1925

Rodchenko obviously intended the kiosk to be free standing. This assumption is supported by the facts that the large billboard above the building is at an angle to the façade and the flags at the top of the mast are placed all around the circumference. Furthermore, an inscription on the drawing, referring to a clock with faces on three sides, corroborates our assumption. Besides the clock, the inscription mentions a projector for advertisements, hanging posters, a screen, a speaker's platform, and finally a place for the sale of books and newspapers. A human figure on the sheet gives an idea of the size of the kiosk.

In Rodchenko's mind the news kiosk developed into a perfectly equipped compact publicity centre which, set up in the right place, might have been very successful. In the dynamic composition and the plasticity of the architectural forms, amplified by glaring colours, Rodchenko expressed the spirit of the age, the vibrant atmosphere of everyday life in revolutionary Russia.

Designed in full awareness of all the utilitarian, aesthetic and ideological factors involved, the kiosk has the further merit of exemplifying Rodchenko's characteristic avoidance of impracticable detail. The structure could have been built easily and quickly with inexpensive materials.

Rodchenko's *News Kiosk* is a Constructivist work, despite the fact that representatives of rigid, dogmatic Constructivism have censured it for being decorative. The structure is indeed decorative, but not as a result of the introduction of unnecessary ornamental elements. The aesthetic quality lies in the arrangement of functional parts with due consideration to the general 'pictorial-sculptural' effect. Furthermore, in this case the decorative appearance is actually dictated by the kiosk's public function itself. It is Rodchenko's special strength that he never became a slave to 'construction for construction's sake'. He possessed the ability to take the principles and results of his 'laboratory' experiments with abstract constructions and compositions and subordinate them to the creative requirements of a functional object.

It is regrettable that certain critics and art historians, who on the whole have shown understanding of and sympathy for the Constructivists, repeat, although in slightly milder terms, the accusations levelled against the Productivists in the 1920s and early 1930s. It was claimed then that the Productivists were incorrigible formalists who endeavoured to compensate for their 'lack of creative perspective' and for the 'exhaustion of their ideological reserves' by taking refuge in making 'objects': in short, that they tried to continue their formalist practice behind the mask of the artist-constructor. This opinion was chiefly supported by alluding to their militant manifestos and slogans as 'Leftist platitudes' and by deriding them for a strong penchant for unrealizable, fantastic constructions.

There were certainly militant slogans and Leftist platitudes, but these were produced partly as a means of self-defence, as a manifestation of the struggle fought for their cause. There were fantastic projects too, but not many, and it was good that such works emerged. On the other hand, numerous plans and concepts were put forward which were completely realistic, practicable and useful, though at the time various reasons precluded their realization. Indeed, what the Productivists achieved in a period of ten years was of epoch-making significance. They produced modern objects suitable for use in a democratic community, and it is a tribute to their art that at the 1925 International Exhibition in Paris visitors considered them harbingers of a new social system.

In 1921 Rodchenko had good reasons to regard further research in the sphere of 'pure art' as hopeless. His susceptibility to what was new constantly drove him on, preventing him not only from repeating himself, but also from dwelling on the elaboration of aspects of technique and form. Having accepted Non-Objective art, he felt it unthinkable to return to representational painting. The fertile period devoted intensively to problems of colour and form was followed by 'black-white-and-grey' works in which colour was 'dead'. The 'brushstroke', i.e. tonal painting, was over for Rodchenko. Finally, in September 1921, he exhibited three monochromatic panels, a red, a yellow, and a blue one, at the '5 × 5 = ·25' exhibition.

With these panels the artist came to the end of his research in easel painting, including Non-Objective art. The train of thought which induced Rodchenko to paint these panels had its own logic:

It is expedient to paint all existing level surfaces in one colour without representing on them any form whatsoever, the level surface being itself a form. . . . In dealing with these panels I maintain that it is only from the margin of a new surface or from the edges in case of forms, that we have a right to use another colour and texture. For instance, a cube may be painted in six colours, every side in a different one.

Thus Rodchenko logically exhausted the theoretical and practical possibilities of purist painting.

The exhibition '5 × 5 = 25' was the last in which members of the older generation of the Russian avant-garde participated together. Five artists — Rodchenko, Stepanova, Vesnin, Popova and Exter — each showed five works; Rodchenko's contributions were the three coloured panels and two drawings, *Line* and *Cubes*. Most of the works on show came under the heading of 'laboratory art', a concept which Popova explains in her catalogue note: 'All these are pictorial compositions and may be assessed only as experiments preparing for the production of concrete, material constructions.'

Rodchenko came to accept the slogan condemning easel painting to death without reservation, as something self-evident (although he was to resume painting in the 1930s). In 1927, in an account of his own work published in No. 6 of the journal *Novii Lef*, he calmly remarked:

When I look at the multitude of pictures I painted in the past I sometimes wonder what to do with them. It would be a pity to burn them, for they are the work of ten years. They are as unnecessary as a church building. No good for anything on earth.

Mayakovsky & Rodchenko, Advertisement Constructors

As was to be expected, the Productivists' intention of being 'linked with production in an organized way' met with numerous obstacles from the outset. The worst difficulties were surely due to the technical backwardness of the country and the lack of means and materials. The conditions were felt primarily in industrial design and in architecture. As regards other fields of design — furniture, books, textiles, the manufacture of objects of everyday use — there were also serious difficulties for want of a competent, well-organized institution to act as an intermediary between the artists and industry. This helplessness and lack of comprehension barred the way for the artists even where their cooperation was welcome.

At the beginning there were two channels connecting the artists with firms: state competitions and individual initiative, i.e. artists showing their readiness to accept commissions. A characteristic case will illustrate the situation: It was reported by the Journal *Vestnik Iskusstv* (*Art Gazette*) that

At Inkhuk Comrade Arvatov said, among other things, that Tatlin, the painter and master of Corner-reliefs, made an offer to the engineers of a machine industry trust to teach the pupils of the factory school as well as the workers how to process material. The engineers failed to grasp the essence of his offer and advised Comrade Tatlin to go to the technical office and teach draughtsmen how to trace fine lines.[24]

At the beginning Rodchenko could only occasionally obtain commissions for applied art. In 1921 and 1922 he put his powers to the test in the theatre, in films and in typography, also taking part in competitions for emblems, trade marks and utilitarian articles. In this early stage of Rodchenko's Productivist activities it soon became evident that his versatility was not forced on him by circumstances, but was a basic trait of his talent. He did everything with enthusiasm, interest and originality; all his works, whether emblems, posters, working clothes, tea-sets or trays, bear the individual hall-marks of his style [75–79].

The first field in which Rodchenko took part on a regular basis was commercial advertising and typography. He began working in these areas early in 1923. This new sphere of interest brought with it close creative collaboration with Mayakovsky, who wrote of Soviet commercial advertising:

We well know the power of propaganda. Nine tenths of the victories in the war and of our economic successes were due to the effectiveness and strength of our propaganda. . . . Advertising is industrial and commercial propaganda. . . . This weapon, commercial propaganda, cannot be left in the hands of NEP [New Economic Policy] men and foreign bourgeois elements.

Meanwhile Rodchenko was struggling on his own:

I had a great deal of trouble with the copy, which was long, dull and uninteresting. I used to correct it myself, and it was not easy to persuade clients to shorten it. Once, for instance, I was given this sentence: 'Those who are not shareholders in Dobrolyet are not citizens of the Soviet Union.' This is neither a rhyme nor a slogan. Volodia

[Mayakovsky], who happened to see it, began to laugh and scoff at it. That made me angry and I told him if good poets just laughed at poor copy, there would never be any good advertisements. After pondering over my words he admitted that I was right – that is how our collaboration began.

Our trade-mark was *Mayakovsky & Rodchenko, Advertisement Constructors*. We worked with immense enthusiasm. These were the first true Soviet advertisements which turned against the little heads, flowers, and other petty bourgeois tawdriness in vogue in the NEP period.

In just under two years Rodchenko and Mayakovsky produced approximately fifty posters, nearly one hundred signs, designs for wrapping-paper, sweet-papers and neon signs, as well as illustrated advertisements for newspapers, journals, and magazines [80–101]. They worked for GUM, Mosselprom, Gosizdat, Rezinotorg[25] and for trade unions. The advertised articles included cigarettes, sweets, biscuits, bread, electric light bulbs, macaroni, butter, galoshes, sausages, beer, share issues, books and many other things.

The scope of Mayakovsky and Rodchenko's advertising activity went far beyond advertising the products of state-owned firms. The poet and the artist also made propaganda in the interest of technical development, improved working conditions, and a cultured existence:

I wrote a poem about a dummy, 'Ready to suck till old age comes.' This text roused indignation, but let me tell you, as long as dirty rags are stuffed into the mouths of children in the country, propaganda to spread the use of dummies is also propaganda in the interest of a healthy generation and for civilization [84].

In the 30 March 1924 issue of *Pravda* (*Truth*) is the following item:

On Mosselprom's orders Mayakovsky and Rodchenko have made pictures and propaganda rhymes for sweet-wrappers. The planned series were 'Leaders of the Revolution', 'Industrialization' and 'Red Moscow'. These sweets are popular mainly in the provinces. The significance of the series from the point of view of propaganda is shown not only by the two-line rhymes, but also by the fact that the previous names of sweets and pictures have been replaced by new ones which clearly expressed the efforts of the Soviet Republic towards revolutionary industrialization, since the taste of the masses is formed not only by, say, Pushkin, but also by the pattern of wallpapers and sweet-wrappers.

The plain, lucid style of Rodchenko's illustrations was in full harmony with Mayakovsky's catchy, laconic, punning two-line rhymes. Texts and pictures were succinct, devoid of unnecessary information. Both had to pay particular attention to clarity, because most of those who looked at posters were still illiterate or semi-literate and had had hardly any visual experience. By the simplest possible means the attention of passers-by had to be drawn to the poster and held until the information was absorbed. Rodchenko achieved this by exploiting the intrinsic features of poster art. He used large, plain, easily legible letters, and often extra large exclamation points and question marks, in order to make the poster more attractive. Arrows in the composition draw the viewer's attention to the meaning of the poster. Symmetrical disposition of letters and other graphic elements as well as accurate representation of the goods advertised were used to the same purpose.

Having abandoned 'little heads', flowers and other ornamentation, Rodchenko endeavoured to expose in his composition the decoration latent in simple accessory graphic elements and colours. In every poster he used variations of black, white and red, one of the most effective colour schemes in poster art. Because of the expense of the printing procedures, Rodchenko could only rarely use photographs for his posters; but when he did the posters became exceptionally suggestive.

Besides printed posters and signboards, Rodchenko produced hand-printed posters for shop windows. He also made pictures for projected street advertisements. In the autumn of 1923 he carved four wooden figures which were put on the top of a paling in a Moscow street along with Mayakovsky's rhymes advertising sweets. Some amusing and engaging little coloured goblins cut out of cardboard were used in witty advertisements for books [96–98].

Rodchenko's memoirs describe the end of this feverishly creative period:

The work was then interrupted. Of course the company assembled in Rapp and Mapp did their utmost to persecute us and seized every opportunity to disparage our work and to stop our activities. Finally they succeeded. Actually they had good grounds for uneasiness – the whole of Moscow, all the stalls and shops of Mosselprom, every newspaper and all the journals were full of our advertisements. . . . Advertising gradually returned to old ways. First pretty female heads and little flowers reappeared; secondly, with the approval of Akhrr, designs such as those representing processions and whole agricultural cooperatives appeared on material for clothing with increasing frequency, until the use of such motifs reached the point of absurdity.[26]

Collage, photomontage and typography

Collage was another field in which Rodchenko proved to be an analytical and consistent purist. He made his first pure collage in 1919 (pure as opposed to Cubist collages, in which application was supplementary to painting) and his last in 1922. By 1919 pure collage was two or three years old, dating back to the activity of the Dadaists. Considering the historical circumstances, however, it is quite possible that Rodchenko knew nothing at that time about Dadaist collage, and relied instead on the local traditions of Cubist collage and on his own experience. He had come across the technique of application in Kazan, and had encountered Cubist collage soon after his arrival in Moscow.

There are at least three types of pure collage: 1. *Representational* collage consists of pictures or details of drawings cut out of periodicals, magazines, encyclopaedias, etc. creating a new graphic medium with its own content, message and symbolism. (This type includes, for example, the work of Max Ernst.) 2. In another type of representational collage newspaper cuttings which represent nothing in themselves are used to create compositions depicting landscapes, still-lifes, etc. 3. In abstract collage, abstract compositions are created from non-representational elements, either used by themselves or in combination with details of drawings and photographs (or newspaper and magazine cuttings).

With few exceptions, Rodchenko's collages belong to the third group [102–04]. Their connection with the artist's 1918–19 Suprematist and Non-Objectivist works is clear. Contrary to the Dadaists, Rodchenko did not see collage as a means of shocking the public or provoking painters. Although exotic, collage was still an 'object' to him. He did not play with material or look down on it. In his hands newspaper cuttings became a medium no less significant than a paint brush or pencil, and every single collage motif, just as in 'real painting', was the result of intentional creative effort. Respecting the purity of the material, Rodchenko never drew or painted on his compositions. The black stripe is the only alien, non-specific element in any of his collages, and this he used to subdue colour in the coloured works, to underline the many layers, or to function as a counter-axis.

Rodchenko's collages are abstract, yet not fully so. The sparingly applied architectural motifs, details of the human figure, etc., convey conceptual and emotional information in addition to fulfilling their formal constructive function. To cite an example: part of the woman's portrait in one of his 1919 collages is covered by a blue-grey stripe bearing the inscription 'Everything for War'; red patches appear in the stripe, as if left there by chance, and the whole fragile construction is broken up by powerful black stripes, two of which form a cross [104]. Thus deeper analysis of the composition – seemingly abstract at first glance – reveals that it has a theme, relating to anti-war propaganda.

In 1920 Rodchenko made a few collage illustrations for I. Aksyonov's *Pillars of Hercules*. The book was never published, but Rodchenko's experiment is noteworthy as one of the first such attempts in that field.

Rodchenko's change from collage to photomontage was, to a certain extent, natural, as photomontage was certainly conceived in the womb of collage. But he and other Soviet Constructivists did not start from scratch in their photomontage work. By the 1920s, photography had reached maturity; it was breaking into the fields of advertising, posters and printing and ousting the traditional graphic artist. This process was particularly marked in the United States and in Germany. Finally, by the beginning of the 1920s, John Heartfield in Berlin was developing collage into photomontage. The renewal of photography was relatively slow in Russia, although this was somewhat compensated for by the rapid development of film, especially newsreels and propaganda films in 1920–22.

In 1922 Alexei Gan launched the first publication of the Russian Constructivists – a periodical entitled *Kino-Fot.* This paper carried on a steadfast struggle against films based on psychological motifs, opposing them with the *kinochestvo* (film eye) philosophy. According to the interpretation given in issue No. 5, *kinochestvo* represents the outlook of a mechanical eye scrutinizing reality from a new angle and with a keener sight than that of man. Mayakovsky's views on the role of cinema appeared in issue No. 4:

For you films are a spectacle, for me they are practically an attitude to life. Films convey movement. Films have a reforming effect on literature. Films destroy aesthetic values. Films mean courage. Films mean sport. Films are a means of spreading ideologies.

Gan involved a few Productivist artists, among them Rodchenko and Stepanova, in his paper. With the exception of two numbers, the covers were designed by Rodchenko, whose artistic products, spatial constructions, Non-Objective compositions and collages were also regularly reproduced in the magazine.

The covers of *Kino-Fot* were made from a combination of print and photographs, and their novelty was that their poster-like appearance, their asceticism, and their conscious effort to be prosaic made them good examples of early Constructivism. On one of the covers Rodchenko included a photograph of Mayakovsky in his leading role in the film *Man Was Not Born to Make Money*, based on Jack London's *Martin Edel* [108]. It is typical that on the front cover of the fifth number of *Kino-Fot* was a photograph of Edison, who in the eyes of the Russian Constructivists personified the technical revolution. Page six of the third number contained drawings by Stepanova with a text by Rodchenko in which he gave a specific Constructivist formula for the future:

LENIN   AND   EDISON
Communism   and   Technology

Experience in collage helped Rodchenko develop quickly in the field of photomontage. A few months after his first attempts, he had fully mastered the technique and the expressive possibilities. This can be seen in the eleven individual illustrations he made between 21 April and 5 June 1932 for Mayakovsky's collection of poetry, *About This* [109–19].

It was no coincidence that Mayakovsky asked Rodchenko to design and illustrate *About This* (*Pro eto*). The poet and the artist were in close contact in Lef (*Levii Front Iskusstva* – Left Front of Art) which Mayakovsky had organized. The launching of the Lef group's magazine called for the appointment of a responsible art editor. The choice fell on Rodchenko. According to Neznamov, secretary of the group, the election took place as follows:

For the cover of the first issue the group conducted a house-competition with Lavinsky, Rodchenko, and Palmov as candidates. The best cover design was submitted by Rodchenko. It was the one chosen by Mayakovsky, too. From then on Rodchenko made the covers for all the issues of *Lef* and later of *Novii Lef*.[27]

He also designed covers for Mayakovsky's volume *Mayakovsky Smiles, Mayakovsky Laughs, Mayakovsky Mocks* [107]. In the 1920s he produced covers for at least ten of Mayakovsky's volumes besides *About This*. They included: *Go to Heaven Yourself* (1925), *Paris* (1925), *Spain, Oceania, Havana, Mexico, America* (1926), *Discovering America* (1926) [129], *To Sergei Yesenin* (1926) [135], *Syphilis* (1926), *Conversation with a Tax Inspector about Poetry* (1926), *Collected Works* (1928–29), *Bed Bug* (1929).

Commenting on *About This*, Mayakovsky wrote:

It was inspired by personal experience and dealt with our common way of life; ... the backbone of the poem is our style of living which has not changed in the least and is now our most dangerous enemy, for it is turning us into Philistines.

With its eiderdowns, bed bugs, samovars, personal domesticity and pink picture frames, this style of life represented, for Mayakovsky, a savage mockery of man, of love, and of the Revolution. The vital importance of this theme, and of Mayakovsky's polemical poetry, raised new demands on the illustrator. It was natural for Rodchenko to use photomontage for this purpose, since the life-like authenticity and documentary character of this type of illustration suited the theme, its ideology and its poetic images much better than traditional illustration. The advantages inherent in this form were enhanced by a high standard of design. Rodchenko's illustrations were cut and glued by hand; technically perfect, they reflect the essence of the poetic work accurately, if not literally. We may without any exaggeration speak of Rodchenko's photomontage illustrations and Mayakovsky's works as perfectly matched in inspiration. Even after fifty years the photomontages are better than any other solution ever adopted for the illustration of the revolutionary poet's works.

The poem *About This* contains no ideal situations to be illustrated; it is a single intense flow of thoughts and feelings, an excited monologue addressed to an imagined public – his contemporaries and the citizens of the thirtieth century. Rodchenko captured the tension and the vivid ideas of the poem by condensing the compositional elements in his illustrations. Condensation does not mean overcrowding in this case; the linking of the chosen details is always justified both aesthetically (silhouettes, contrast of forms, rich variety of white, grey and black, and so on) and from the point of view of content.

In terms of technique, Rodchenko's illustrations to Sergei Tretyakov's unpublished children's book *Samozvery*, designed jointly with Stepanova in 1926, are masterly and exhilarating, but difficult to classify as any specific form of art; the term 'photographic illustrations' can be accepted only conditionally, for lack of a more fitting name [137–43].

The photogram (no-camera) technique did not attract him then or later, though he was undoubtedly acquainted with it and used it experimentally. In the early 1920s he gave a short series of talks at Vkhutein (Fine Arts Technical School) on photography. Urusevsky (the cameraman for the film *Cranes on the Wing*) was present and reported:

We were very disappointed to find that Rodchenko seemed to have forgotten to bring a camera. He took us into the laboratory, put a white sheet of paper on the table and shed light on it with a lamp from one side. He placed a few objects between the source of light and the sheet of paper, so that they threw shadows on the latter. He then replaced the ordinary sheet by photographic paper, and after making a short exposure, developed the picture. A peculiar composition appeared. ... In this simple manner he acquainted us with the basic elements of photography, an art with an expressive force and a plasticity of its own.

The peculiar composition mentioned by Urusevsky was a photogram.

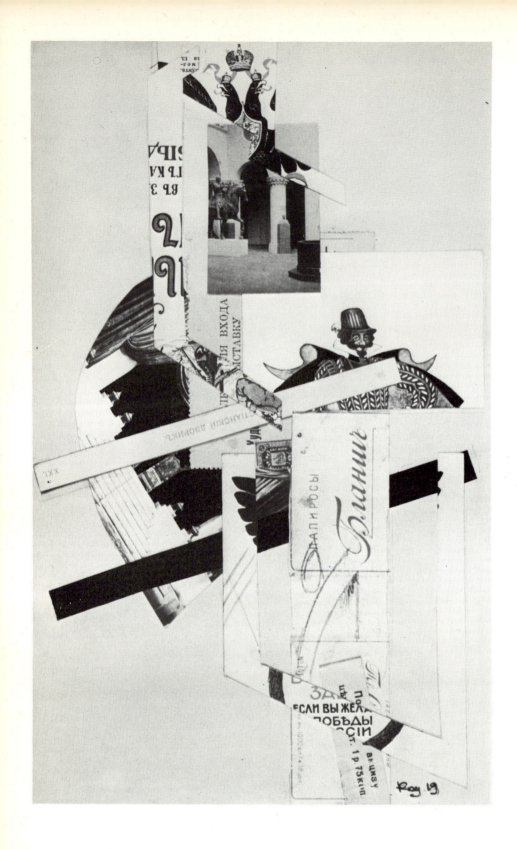

103–04 *Collages* 1919

105 Rodchenko and his wife Varvara Stepanova 1922

106 *Mayakovsky Silhouette* 1939

СКЛАД ИЗДАНИЙ:

Москва, Леонтьевский пер., 23

107 Cover (back and front) for *Mayakovsky Smiles, Mayakovsky Laughs, Mayakovsky Mocks* 1923

МАЯКОВСКИЙ
УЛЫБАЕТСЯ
МАЯКОВСКИЙ
СМЕЕТСЯ
МАЯКОВСКИЙ
ИЗДЕВАЕТСЯ

КИНО
–ФОТ N 4

Цена 75 руб.

МАЯКОВСКИЙ

Родченко.

НЕ
ДЛЯ
ДЕНЕГ
родив
шийся
КИНО
по
РОМАНУ
ДЖЕКА
ЛОНДОНА
МАРТИН
ИДЭН

109 Cover for Mayakovsky's *About This* 1923

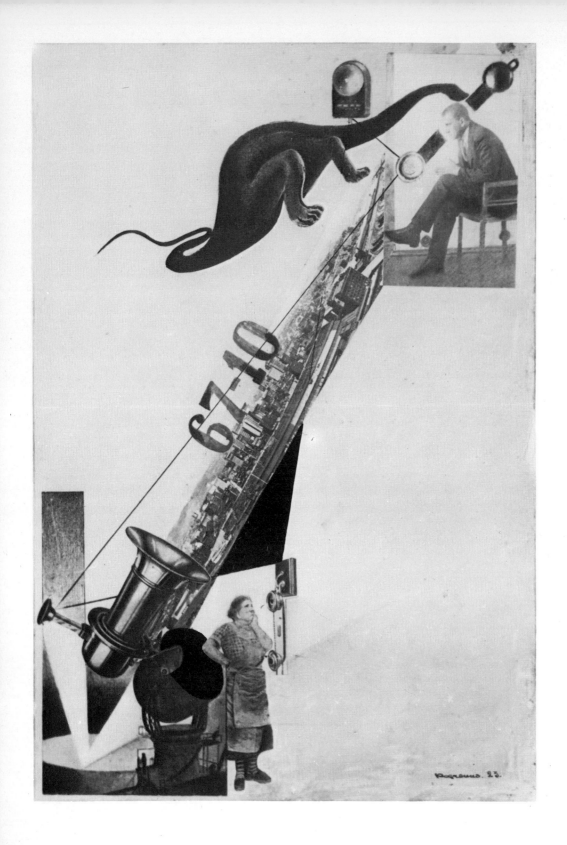

110–11 Photomontages for Mayakovsky's *About This* 1923

116–17 Photomontages for Mayakovsky's *About This* 1923

141

МАРТ 1

19 ▪ МОСКВА ▪ 23

ЖУРНАЛ

ЛЕВОГО ФРОНТА

ИСКУССТВ

ИЗДАТЕЛЬ: ГОСИЗДАТ

ОТВЕТСТВЕННЫЙ РЕДАКТОР

В. В. МАЯКОВСКИЙ

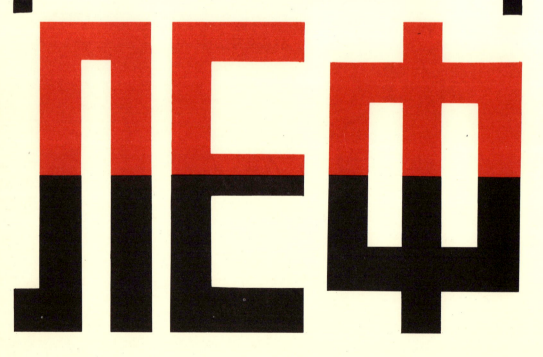

№ 6

новый

леф

ГОСИЗДАТ

1927

122–23 *Red Army Manoeuvres* 1927

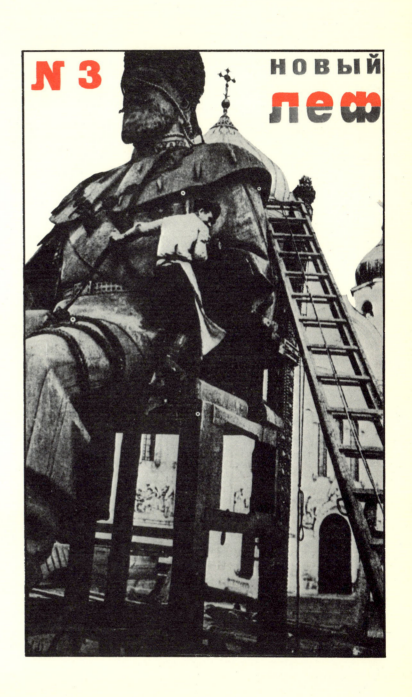

125 Cover for *Novii Lef* 1927

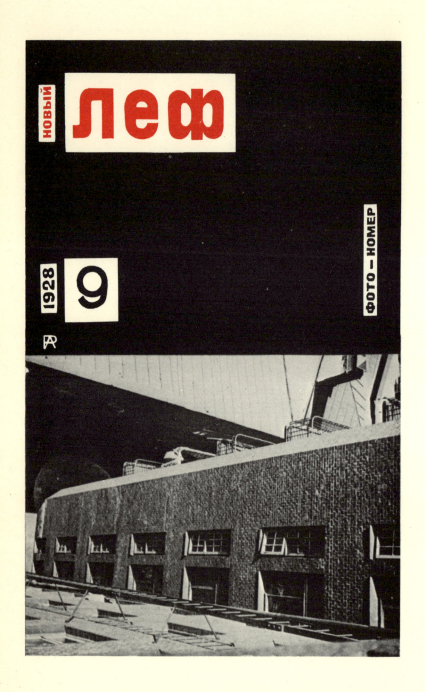

126 Cover for *Novii Lef* 1928

127   Cover for Marietta Sanginyan's *Jim Dollar* 1924

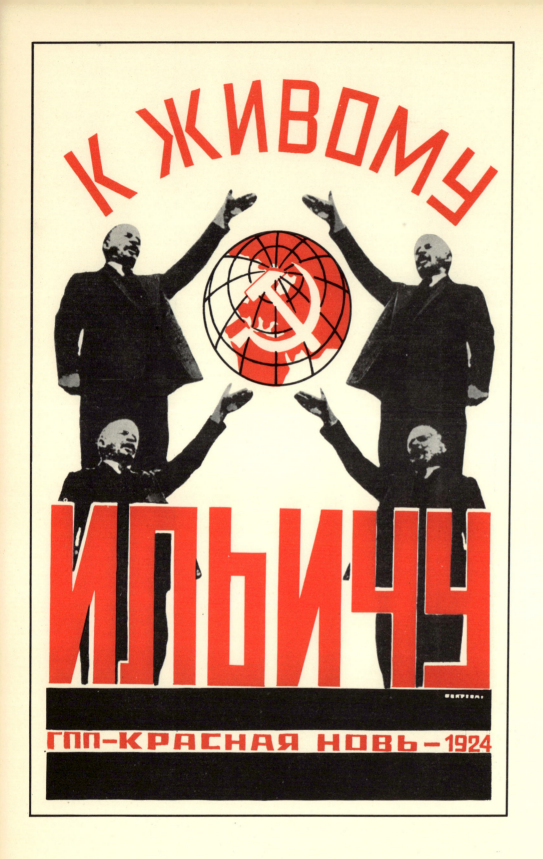

128 Cover for *Towards the Living Ilyich* 1924

МАЯКОВСКИЙ

мое

Открытие

Америки

1926

ГОСУДАРСТВЕННОЕ ИЗДАТЕЛЬСТВО

129 Cover for Mayakovsky's *Discovering America* 1926

ПЕТ
АВИО
СТИХИ
К 19 23 Ь
КРАСНАЯ НОВЬ

А Р.

132 Cover for *Radioslushatel* 1929
133 Cover for *The Soviet Union in Construction* 1936

За Рубежом № 2 АВГУСТ 1930

СМОТРИТЕ!
ВО СЛАВУ
СВОЕЙ ДИКТАТУРЫ
ДЕТЕРДИНГ и РОКФЕЛЛЕР „СПАСАЮТ" КУЛЬТУРУ

Фото-монтаж А. Родченко

134 Cover for *Za Rubezhom* 1930
135 Cover (back and front) for Mayakovsky's *To Sergei Yesenin* 1926

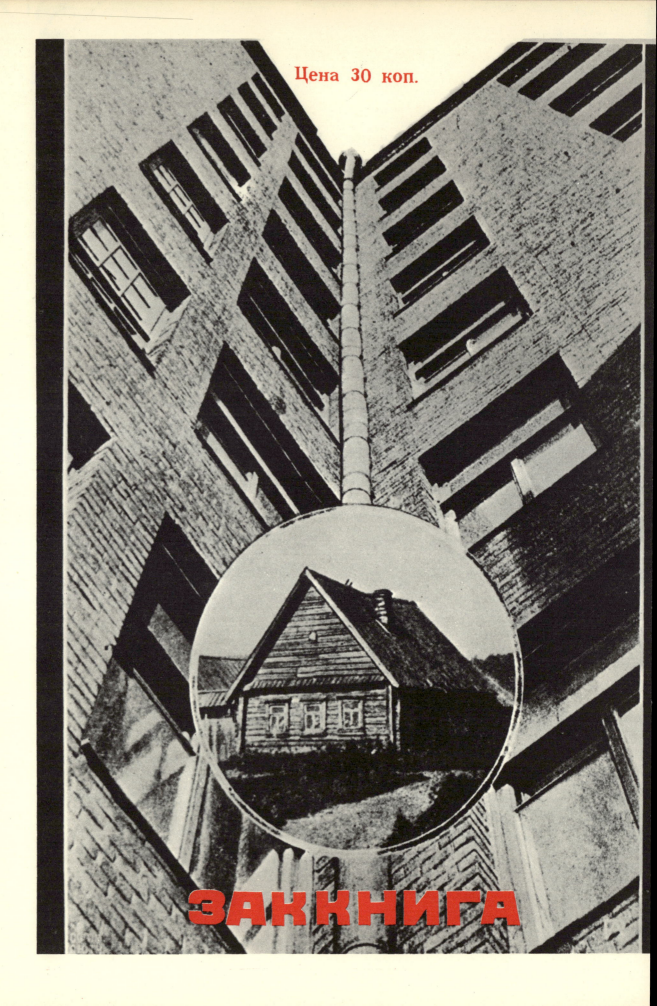

Цена 30 коп.

ЗАККНИГА

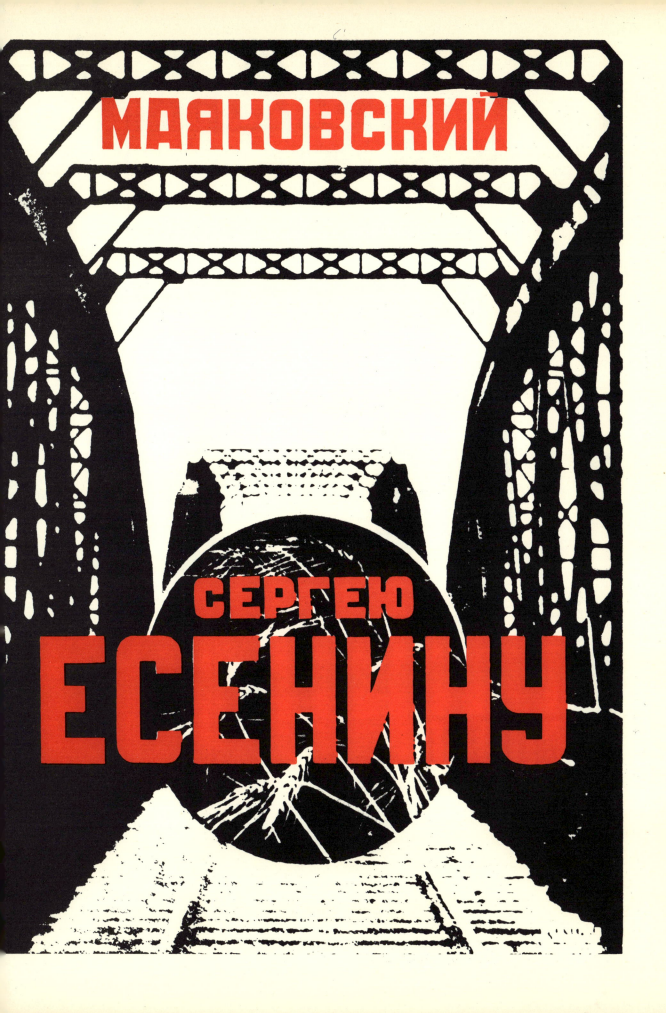

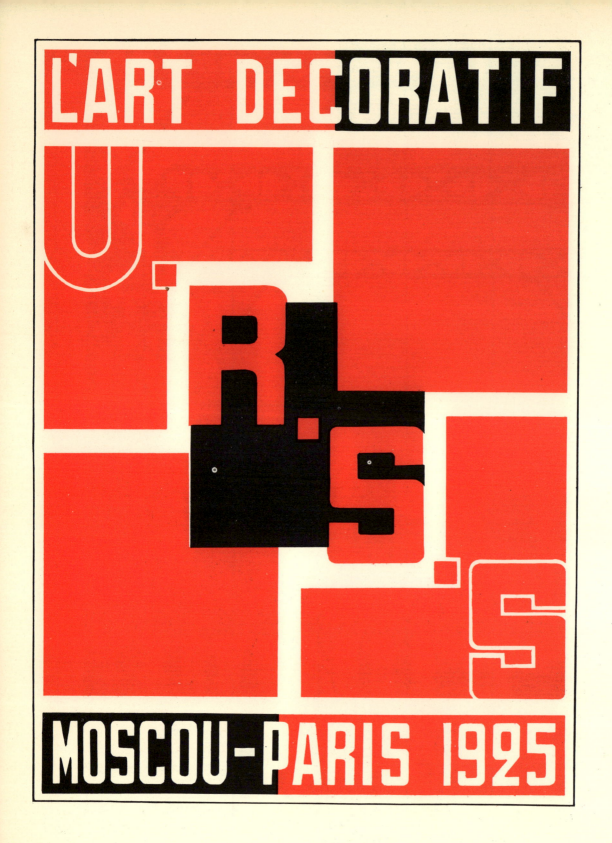

136 Catalogue cover for 'Art Deco' Paris Exhibition 1925

161   137 Photographic illustration for Sergei Tretyakov's unpublished verses for children 1926

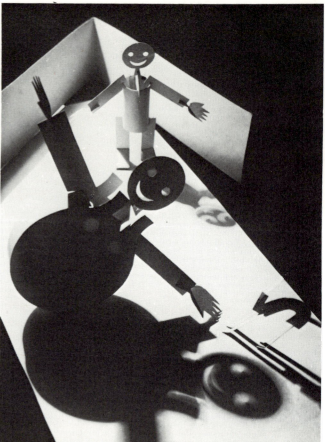

138–41 Photographic illustrations for Sergei Tretyakov's unpublished verses for children 1926

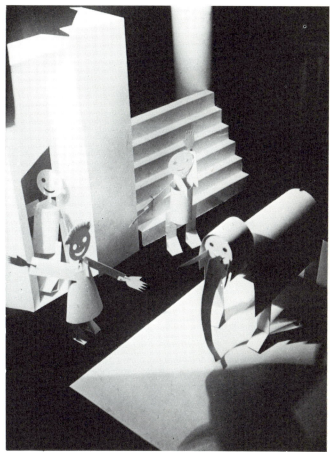

 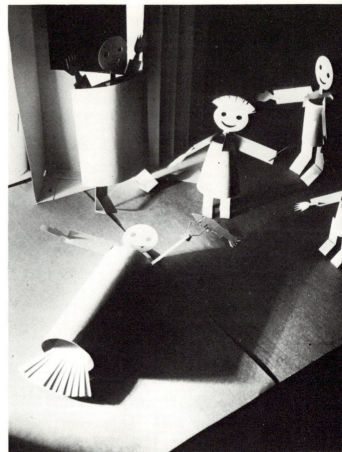

142–43 Photographic illustrations for Sergei Tretyakov's unpublished verses for children 1926

Alexander Rodchenko is the classic figure in Constructivist cover design. In the 1920s he worked for nearly all the Moscow publishers; as a result he made cover designs for an extremely wide range of books, from poems to scientific and technical literature. His initials may be found on the photomontages of *Molodaya Gvardiya, Sputnik Kommunista, Sovietskoe Kino, Radioslushatel* [132], *Za Rubezhom* [133] and other periodicals, as well as *Lef* and *Novii Lef* [120–21, 126].[28] He was equally successful in both photomontage and purely graphic covers, the latter generally being composed of letters, or letters and patches of colour [107–09].

Rodchenko accepted, though he did not follow dogmatically, the 1920s maxim that books should be made only with the means of the book, that is to say, only with type: 'Minimum cost, maximum appositeness, this is the most important principle.' By this he meant that the appearance of the book should harmonize with the contents. Rodchenko does not use the word 'beauty'; he takes it for granted. Beauty is a law of creation whose unconditional acceptance is the professional duty of the artist [124–36].

Rodchenko was not enthusiastic about purely typographic covers. The use of type answered the demand for 'minimum cost'; but to achieve 'maximum appositeness' and artistic quality with type alone was not easy. Photographs and photomontages can palliate, but cannot completely alleviate, the dryness of type; and often the cover had to consist of lettering only. This, in addition to a poor selection of typefaces and inferior paper and board, led Rodchenko to the decision to work with hand-drawn lettering.

Once he had emancipated himself from the type-case, the designer had much greater scope to add supplementary graphic elements of his own, to contrast positive and negative letters, and to use colour freely. The result: exquisitely balanced, classically composed cover designs which include such masterpieces as the cover design for the Soviet catalogue for 'Art Deco', the 1925 Paris exhibition [136]. Mayakovsky was not under the influence of personal bias when, at the debate entitled 'Lef or Bluff?' on 13 March 1927, he defended Lef and Rodchenko against the attacks of a literary man named Viacheslav Polonsky and spoke appreciatively of Rodchenko's contribution to Soviet graphic design:[29]

In 1923, siding with Lef, and keeping abreast of technical developments, Rodchenko was the first to switch over from pen and pencil drawing to photomontage. This happened in 1923, and now on the basis of a decree, the whole of photo-journalism has to switch to montage illustration as elaborated by Rodchenko. In three years Rodchenko developed a book and cover style proper to the Soviet Union. The best covers – like that of Lenin's *Collected Works* and the catalogue of the Paris exhibition, for example, though they amount to over two hundred in total – are all linked with Rodchenko's name. . . . Look at the recent pages of *Izvestia* and *Pravda*, or, if you are interested in the history of the Communist Party, at the 25 photomontages published by the Communist Academy – the only history of the Communist Party told in pictures – and bear in mind that they are all Rodchenko's own work.[30]

Teacher at Vkhutemas

The resolution passed by the art students' congress held in Petrograd on 24 April 1918 contains the following demand:

In this century, the century of great changes and of the liberation of man, every creative manifestation in the arts and by artists must be absolutely free. ... The essential condition for the existence of a high standard of art being freedom for artistic creation, all centralization and all authority that arbitrarily governs intellectual life is our enemy and will be rejected by us. ... The petty egotism and vanity-breeding of the educational system of the past must be relentlessly eliminated from the schools. Down with diplomas, degrees, decorations and privileges which disgrace art. We demand self-government for the schools, recognition of the leading role of youth in the intellectual life of schools and, implicitly, in artistic life.

The art students' claim to a leading role in artistic life was somewhat premature; their other demands, however, were almost all met. In September 1918, all institutions of higher education in the arts were changed into Free Public Art Studios which every person over the age of sixteen had the right to enter. No school certificate was required from the applicants. Internal democracy in the reorganized educational institutions was ensured by the 'Instructions concerning the choice of teachers at the Free Public Art Studios', which included the following rights for the students:

1. Every student of the Free Public Art Studios, without any exception, has the right to choose his teacher for his chosen subject himself. ... 3. Every trend must have a place in the studios. ... 7. The students of the Free Public Art Studios will form groups according to the trend nearest to their art. ... 10. Provided they have a minimum of twenty members the groups so organized can choose their own teacher, independently of other groups. ... 14. The students are to have the prerogative of working without a master, if they choose to do so. 15. The appointment of the teacher chosen is for two years and is to be approved by the Commissar of Public Education.

The Free Public Art Studios comprised (1) the painting workshops (painting and decoration laboratories with specialized and individual workshops); (2) sculpture studios; (3) architecture workshops; (4) the art research institute.

The first Free Public Art Studios were established in the building of the former Stroganov School of Applied Arts; the second at the site of the School of Painting, Sculpture and Architecture.

The reorganization of artistic education was carried out by Izo. This department initiated the extension of the educational programme to the applied arts. As early as 1920 the activists of Izo held unequivocal views on the aims and character of education in this field. They maintained that the country, recovering from destruction, needed not individual creative artists and decorators but artist-constructors, people able to fit effectively into a modern system of mechanized production or, as an initial step, to take part according to their abilities in the launching of production. The concept of 'painter-decorator', born directly after the Revolution in reaction to the former 'art of the upper classes', was replaced by the concepts of 'artist-constructor' and 'artist-engineer'. By the latter was meant a completely new type of artist, one who successfully united professional knowledge with extensive technical experience. Izo's manifesto included the following statements:

The time approaches when the proletariat will need buildings accommodating tens of thousands. These will have to be built with minimal effort, minimal material and maximum strength. Such demands can only be met by highly qualified artist-workers working according to a coordinated scheme and with the use of every feat of modern engineering. . . . The design laboratories must not employ materials alien to production, only to transfer their design mechanically to another material later. False conceptions of artistic forms independent of material arise only if the designer fails to adopt a positive attitude towards material.

In June 1920, the first All-Russian Conference of Institutes of Fine Arts and Studios of Applied Arts was convened. The participants discussed and accepted suggestions for the widening of the technical training conducted at art schools. It was decided to unite the first and second Free Public Art Studios in Moscow into a single Academy of Fine Arts. A fairly large number of artists who had actively cooperated in the reformation of the curricula of the academy were invited to teach at the reorganized Free Studios. Most of them, like Rodchenko, Popova, Vesnin, Udaltsova, Drevin and others, were members of Inkhuk.

At the end of the same year, probably by virtue of the resolution of the People's Commissariat of OSSSK published on 25 December 1920, the Free Studios were renamed Advanced Art-Technical Workshops (Vkhutemas). According to a resolution signed by Lenin, Vkhutemas was to be a special advanced technical-industrial institution designed to train highly qualified artist-experts for industry. In ten years Vkhutemas (from 1926 onwards called Vkhutein, or Fine Arts Technical School) developed into an elaborate institution with a highly heterogeneous scope of activity. It was dissolved in the spring of 1930, and its different faculties were reorganized into independent colleges: the College of Architecture, the College of Typography, and the Faculty of Art of the Textile Industrial College. The faculties of painting and sculpture became departments of the Academy of Fine Arts.

Rodchenko's memoirs contain the following comments on Vkhutemas:

In 1920 I started my career as teacher at Vkhutemas. Until the dissolution of this institution in 1930, I was professor and dean of the faculty of metalwork. This faculty began its work on virgin soil, and what was even worse, it was housed in the handicraft workshop of the former Stroganov School, used for the production of devotional objects for the church. . . . Here I set myself the task of training constructors specialized in the artistic-technical working of metal, including the production of metal fittings for the interior of motor cars and aeroplanes. They were to be constructor-artists full of creative initiative and equipped with technical knowledge.

It was a hard battle we fought, for the new type of constructor-artist who had no precedent in Czarist Russia. After completing their courses, the students of the metalwork faculty started work as constructors, section-heads or technical managers.

Rodchenko both taught and learned during this period. The experience he had gained while working at Izo's Sub-Section for Applied Arts proved most valuable to him as did the work he performed jointly with members of Zhivskulptarkh. Furthermore, Inkhuk had had a beneficial intellectual effect on him. Like other Productivists, Rodchenko owed a great deal to Mayakovsky, who gave his comrades both moral support and, often, material assistance. According to Rodchenko's reminiscences, 'He did not hoard anything. What he brought with him [from abroad] – posters, catalogues, brochures, pictures of scenery, photos of stage settings and buildings – he distributed among us.' He also gave valuable assistance to Productivist professors by personally visiting the studios, where he agitated for Productivist art, exciting and mobilizing the students of Vkhutemas, in whose eyes he enjoyed great prestige.

The Rodchenko of those years is remembered by Galina Chichagova, one of the students who joined the Free Studios in 1920:

First lesson. A man, whose appearance resembled that of a pilot or a chauffeur, entered the classroom. His clothes, a beige jacket and grey-green knee-breeches, looked like a soldier's uniform. He wore black boots and grey leggings, and a black cap with a shiny leather peak on his head. His face was very pale but had regular features. I noticed at once that he was a new, different type of man. His manner of speech and behaviour was not like a teacher's at all. . . . Once he took us to the Polytechnic Museum to hear a lecture on radio broadcasting. It was our first joint excursion. Rodchenko was interested in science and often talked to us about scientific subjects. . . .

During our further meetings with Rodchenko we became more and more convinced that he was a man with an individual and modern concept of the world. Whether we talked of art or everyday subjects, he always held an original view. . . . He gave the impression of a rather quiet, reticent person, yet he radiated the force and determination of the resolute.

Soviet historians are now investigating the history of Vkhutemas and Vkhutein. So far, however, only publications dealing with isolated subjects and problems have appeared: a good many years will pass before it is possible to issue a comprehensive monograph based on a thorough analysis of the problems involved and a systematic elaboration of the documents pertaining to the history of the institute.

Contemporaneous and more recent publications dealing with the educational system and the practical impact of Vkhutemas and Vkhutein give us an insight into certain questions and enable us to draw certain general conclusions. But they have proved insufficient to form an accurate and thorough assessment of the activity of the individual professors, even those who are richly documented. The Rodchenko archive contains a great many gaps at the moment. Nevertheless, the educational programmes drafted by the artist himself permit us to evaluate his more important pedagogic principles. Apart from their other merits, these programmes are of considerable interest for their modernity: the means of teaching artistic construction and the ideas concerning the mastery of artistic design fundamentally correspond to the basic principles in the instruction of designers today.

Galina Chichagova recounts a few details of the first system of instruction adopted by Vkhutemas, as well as a whole series of episodes from the stormy life of the young members of this organization in its initial period. The Advanced Art-Technical Workshops were divided into four classes, preparatory, basic, specialized and advanced, the latter headed by an artist-professor. The basic course had eight subject workshops, each taught by a separate teacher as follows: (1) maximum effect of colour, Popova; (2) form as manifested by colour, Osmyorkin; (3) colour in space, Exter; (4) colour in plane, Kliun; (5) the structure of space in painting, Rodchenko; (6) the simultaneous presence of form and colour, Drevin; (7) dimension in space, Udaltsova; (8) problems of colour and form, Baranov-Rossin. Chichagova continues:

According to the programme, the students had to proceed from subject to subject and become acquainted with the methods of painting covered by the eight subjects in two years. The students were free to choose the studio they desired to work in, and sometimes a student remained in one particular studio throughout his training.

Our [Rodchenko's] studio was often visited by guests from other cities (1921–22) and even by foreigners, who called Vkhutemas an academy and spoke highly of the organization and programme of our instruction. These may have been from the Bauhaus.

At about the time of the foundation of Vkhutemas in 1920–21, the so-called Bogdanovists (who took their name from their leader, Bogdanov) began to revolt. They expressed their dissatisfaction with the basic course, protesting against both its programme and its teachers. Nor did they approve of such professors as Konchalovsky, Maskov, Lentulov, Falk and Shevchenko, in charge of the specialized classes, not to mention Kandinsky, who during these years also taught a class of this grade. . . . A little later students working under Shevchenko, Falk, Maskov, Kuznetsov and the others spoke out against the Vkhutemas curricula and the strongly advocated Productivist art. They defended the aesthetic principles of 'art for art's sake', and we called them Chistoviks. The lower grade remained true to the principles of Productivist art. Many of the students went from studio to studio to agitate in its defense. We fought passionate, wordy battles.

In addition to the Bogdanovists and Chistoviks the Productivists had yet another enemy within their walls: the Prikladniks, or supporters of traditional applied arts. A further circumstance that affected Rodchenko directly is described by Chichagova:

Although Workshop No. 5 still included painting in 1920, we were gradually led to switch over to three-dimensional constructions and functional objects. . . . By the end of the 1921–22 school year the slogans of Productivist art had become very popular, as a result of which students in the faculty of painting began to change studios, going over one after the other to groups pursuing Productivist art. At the end of 1922 our whole group went over to the metalwork studio where Rodchenko had been invited to teach.

The basic course in Vkhutemas, which corresponds to the preparatory classes of present day design colleges, was the pride of the institution from the first.[31] By a common effort the large team of painters, graphic artists, sculptors and architects active there soon elaborated a complex method for the study of the basic principles of graphic and plastic art as well as of colour and spatial form. Its purpose was to acquaint the students of different branches of art with the laws of artistic form, and to develop their faculty of analysis, artistic intuition, creative initiative, imagination and talent for execution.

In its organization and methods the basic course assumed a more or less definite form as early as 1922–23. The earlier eight subjects were replaced by four complex groups of subjects in so-called 'concentres' (*kontsentry*). These were: graphic art, planar-colour, spatial dimension and space formation. The concentre system adopted two programmes: one for first-year students and one for second-year students. The second-year students attended the concentre that corresponded best to the profession they wished to follow: thus, future sculptors, metalworkers, woodworkers and ceramicists attended the concentre for spatial dimensions, architects attended space formation, and the painters, graphic artists and textile designers attended the planar colour and graphic art concentres.

At the 1925 Paris 'Art Deco' exhibition, Vkhutemas was awarded a diploma of honour for its new analytical instructional method, for the curriculum elaborated for the basic course, and for the experimental works put on show, including works by Rodchenko's pupils. In addition to his work in painting, and later as professor and dean of metalwork, Rodchenko taught the basic course, and drew up a number of curricula:

Organizational programme for the painting laboratory at the Public Fine Art Studios

I. The laboratories set up for the study of painting are of a scientific and experimental character.

A. The scientific task of the laboratories is to study and elaborate the professional and technical problems of painting. To this effect experiments are being carried out
(1) in the field of *colour*;
(2) in the field of *form*;
(3) in the laws of *construction*;
(4) in the elaboration of surface texture, called *facture*.

B. The educational objective of the laboratories is to give every student scientific and technical knowledge as well as practical technical experience, independent of his creative personality.

II. The laboratory is divided into specialized *sections* where the various elements of painting, i.e.
(1) colour,
(2) form,
(3) construction,
(4) surface texture,
(5) material,
can be studied.

A. Study of the dynamic and static elements of painting:
(1) Practical and theoretical analysis of the individual elements and basic characteristics;
(2) Analysis of the components of works of art from different periods;
(3) Analysis of the components of objects;
(4) Practical solution of special tasks connected with the characteristics of certain elements.

B. Comparison of components:
(1) Study of the relationship between various elements;
(2) Comparison of elements in works of art;
(3) Practical solution of tasks in connection with such comparisons.

12 December 1920

THE STRUCTURE OF PICTORIAL SPACE
(Theoretical themes)

Pictorial space is formed by reciprocal action between *colour spaces* (or coulisses). Their components are:
(1) line,
(2) plane,
(3) volume,

and their

(1) rhythm,
(2) area,
(3) colour,
(4) surface texture.

1. *The line* may indicate the graphic frame of a pictorial space or mark the limit, crossing point or spatial continuation of planes.

2. *The plane* is a two-dimensional colour space.

3. *Volume* calls for three-dimensional construction, but not necessarily in a sculptural form.

4. The essential character of a construction is determined by its *rhythm* to which all spatial relationships are subordinated.

5. *Colour* not only paints the objects but has a significance of its own and helps to emphasize the spatial relationship between colour surfaces.

6. *Surface texture* determines the character of the superficial part of the picture, gives emphasis to the relationships between different colours and materializes the colour spaces.

1920

PROFESSOR A.M.RODCHENKO'S PROGRAMME FOR METAL OBJECT DESIGN AT THE FACULTY OF WOOD- AND METALWORK

1. Design of objects for the metalwork industry to be constructed in full scale by the students.

A. Single-functional objects.

1. Construction of objects from metal alone. Examples: spoon, door-handle, pot, iron, pair of scissors, horseshoe, etc.

2. Construction of objects with the combined use of metal and other materials. Examples: fork, knife, peg, etc.

B. Multi-functional objects.

1. Construction of objects from metal alone.

2. Construction of objects with the combined use of metal and other materials. Examples: magnifying apparatus for a photo laboratory, writing set, etc.

II. Designs of objects for the metalwork industry to be constructed by the students as models only.

1. Single-functional objects.

2. Multi-functional objects.

III. Designs of objects for the metalwork industry to be drawn by the students.

IV. Artistic finishing of the surface of various objects (materials).

1. Plates for enamelled and etched inscriptions.

2. Badges, coats of arms and signs.

INDUSTRIAL DESIGN

For third and fourth-grade students of the Wood- and Metalwork Faculty of Vkhutemas. Professor A.M. Rodchenko.

Industrial design should develop in future artist-engineers the ability to recognize in a modern object its basic principles of construction and the form as well as the nature of its material.

Specialists engaged in the production of modern objects should be acquainted with as many articles on the market as possible, so that in developing new objects they may make use of, and improve upon, current cultural-technical achievements.

1. Drawing of objects of simple structure presented in class (e.g. penknife, chair).

2. Drawing of objects with only semi-visible structure (e.g. desk, accordion).

3. Drawing of objects with concealed structure (e.g. electric stove, fountain pen).
4. Drawing by memory of ordinary everyday objects (e.g. electric plug, stool).
5. Drawing of objects shown in class for a very short time only.
6. Comprehension of the structure of objects and drawing them from photographs.
7. Drawing of objects during and after excursions.

The Paris Exhibition

This morning I went to my office. Suddenly they descended upon me.
   'Comrade Rodchenko, we want you.'
   'Why? What has happened?'
   'Tomorrow is 1 May. The club has to be decorated. We have an allocation of 200 roubles; we've already prepared the slogans and the material and bought some fir trees.'
   A month passes and it starts all over again. Tomorrow is Aviakhim Day[32] ... 200 roubles ... decoration ... fir trees ... etc.
   At the same time the walls of the club are dirty, the furniture is shabby, the clock broken, and so on.
   Wouldn't it have been better, Comrades, if for 1 May, precisely on the occasion of 1 May, you had bought, say, a dozen chairs?
   Or, on the occasion of Aviakhim Day, had whitewashed the walls?

(A. Rodchenko, *Novii Lef*, 1927, No. 6.)

These instructive lines were written by the artist in *Novii Lef*, No. 6, in 1927: two years after the Paris International Exhibition (Art Deco), where his *Workers' Club* was one of the most remarkable of the Soviet entries. From the pavilion designed by the Constructivist architect Melnikov, to the posters on show, all of the Soviet material was highly successful, both with the public and with the experts. The interior and furniture designs, graphic works, stage scenery, architectural and textile designs, in short, practically everything exhibited by the young Socialist republic, received international recognition. The exhibitors owed their success mainly to their modernity, to their bold ingenious designs, and to the simplicity and practicality of the articles of everyday use; in fact to precisely the features that had so much difficulty gaining acceptance at home.
   It is true that the country was still suffering from shortages of some of the most necessary materials, and that her technical development was still at a very low level. But apart from those factors the major obstacles to the realization of new ideas and conceptions were more often frustration, obstinate attachment to the familiar, the rigid pursuit of long obsolete methods, and poor organization of labour. It may sound paradoxical, yet it is a fact, that the truest industrial design in Russia in the 1920s was not industrial at all but led to the production of unique objects. The preconditions for a design movement that could actively affect the material environment were still absent. Nevertheless, a great deal had been achieved: the Satura hydraulic power station was already in operation; book design and advertising had important results to their credit; the first modern buildings had appeared in the streets of Soviet cities; and last but not least, there was Melnikov's pavilion of glass and wood in Paris. To quote Le Corbusier, it was 'the only pavilion worth seeing in the whole exhibition' [145–47].

144 *Textile Design* 1924

145–46 Workers' Club for the Paris Exhibition 1925

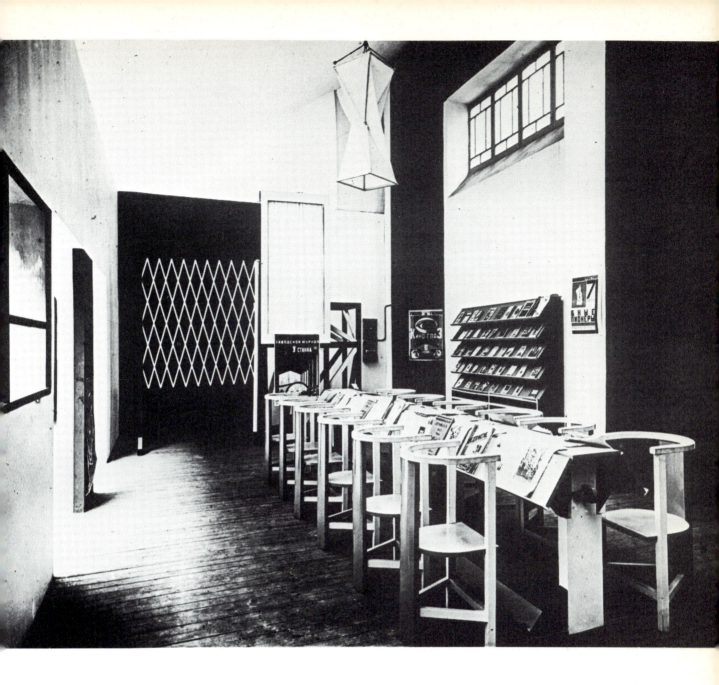

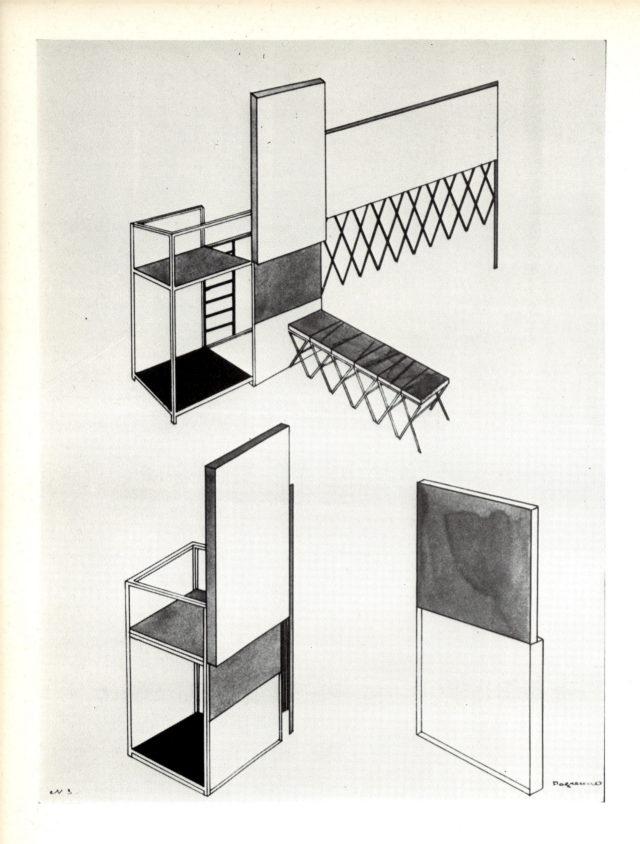

147 *Furniture for the Workers' Club* 1925

148 *Costume Design* 1919

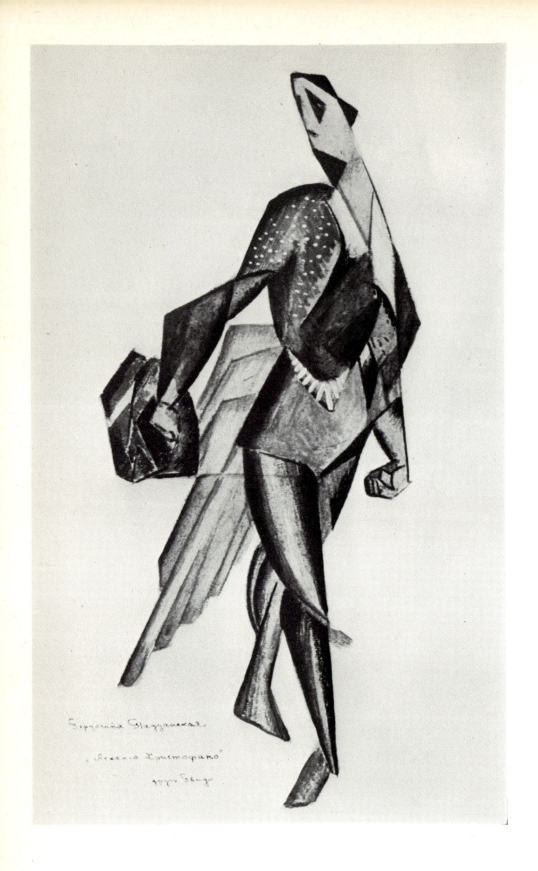

149–50 Costume designs for the play *The Princess of Padua* 1914

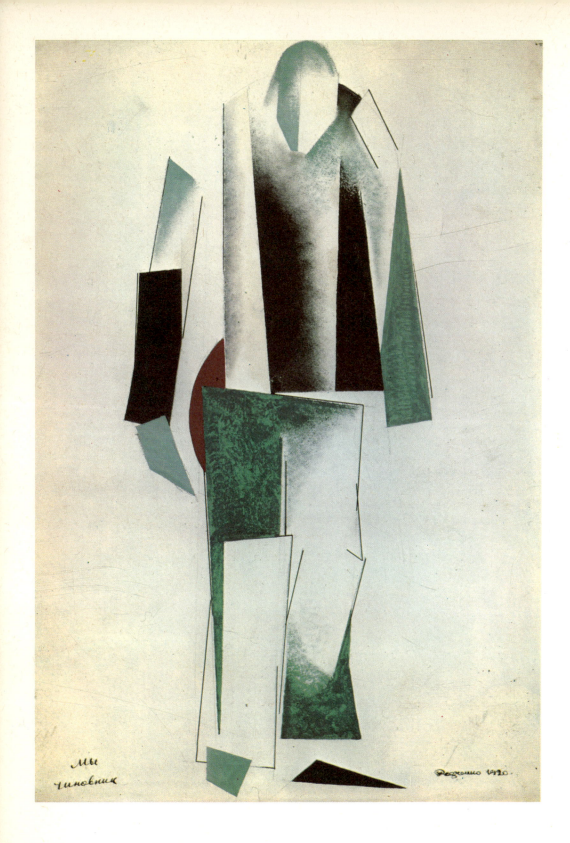

мы
чиновник

Федченко 1920.

151 *Costume Design* 1920

шестая часть МИРА

АВТОР-РУКОВОДИТЕЛЬ
ДЗИГА ВЕРТОВ

1 выпуск.

ПРОИЗВОДСТВО
ГОСКИНО

152 Film poster for *One-sixth of the World* 1926

153–54 Film poster for *Cine-eye* 1924

ГОСКИНО ПРОИЗВОДСТВО ГОСКИНО

КИНО ГЛАЗ

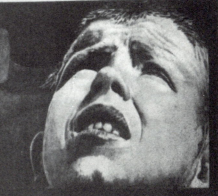

РОДЧЕНКО

6 СЕРИЙ

РАБОТА
ДЗИГИ ВЕРТОВА
ОПЕРАТОР
КАУФМАН

Главлит № 253   Типо-литографія Госкино: ул Коммуны 35. Телеф. 5-75-09.   Тираж 8000.

БРОНЕНОСЕЦ

1905

ПОТЕМКИН

БРОНЕНОСЕЦ

19

ПРОИ
ГОС
ПЕРВОЙ

постановка
С.М. ЭЙЗЕНШТЕЙНА

ПОТЕМКИН

15

...СТВО
...НО
...АБРИКИ

РОДЧЕНКО

ГЛАВНЫЙ ОПЕРАТОР
ЭДУАРД ТИССЭ

158 Scene from the play *The Bed Bug* 1929

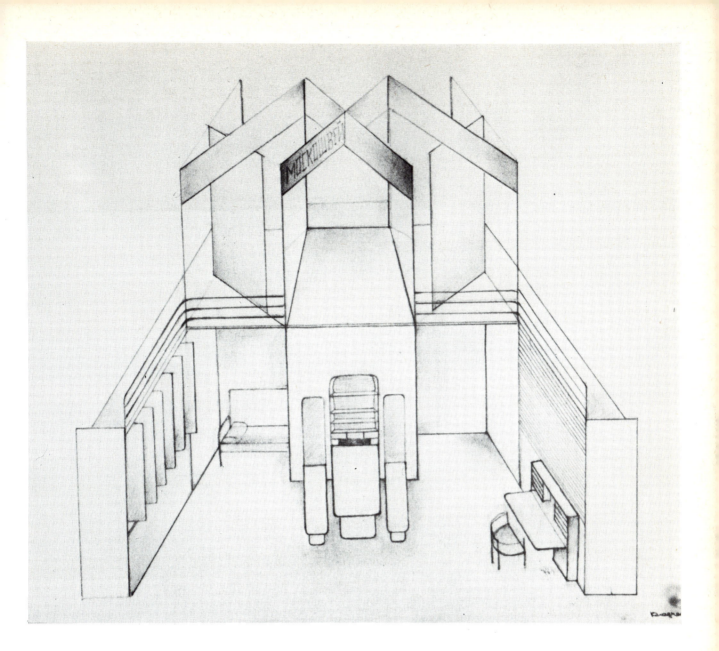

159 Set design for the play *The Pendulum* 1929

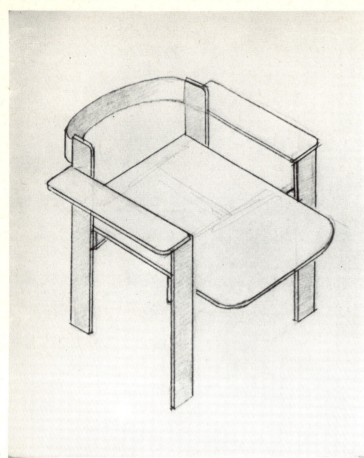

160–61 Furniture designs for
the play *The Pendulum* 1929
162 Costume design for
the play *The Pendulum* 1929
163–65 Costume designs for
the play *The Bed Bug* 1929

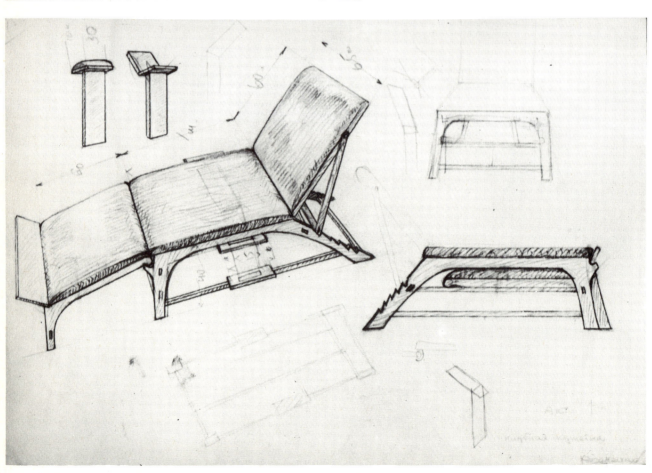

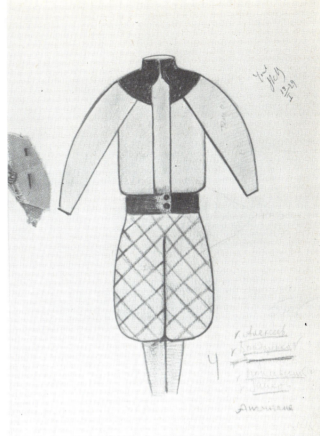

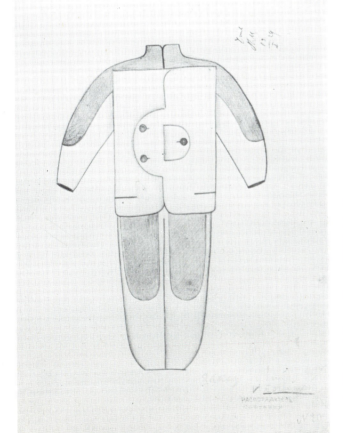

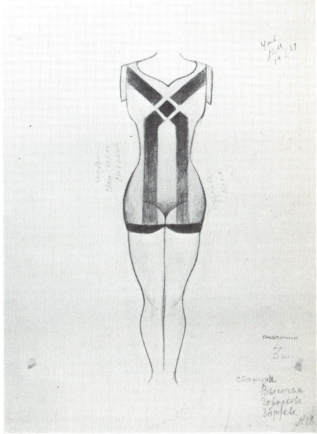

166 Rodchenko, Mayakovsky, Meyerhold and Shostakovich working on
Mayakovsky's play *The Bed Bug* 1929

Rodchenko's *Workers' Club* was a concrete achievement. Its interior constituted an excellent model for an original and rationally designed social establishment. The furniture, all made of wood, consisted of only the most necessary pieces: a table with folding sides, comfortable chairs, shelves for books and periodicals, glass cases on the wall for posters, and a convertible platform for speeches, conferences and performances. Rodchenko said:

It is so simple, clean and bright that people will not leave any litter about, even accidentally. There is a lot of shining Ripolin,[33] white, red and grey, all over the place. The objects do not dominate, but are useful and necessary 'implements', their design subordinated to their function.

Rodchenko designed the furniture of the club to be functional, and even the furniture industry of the 1920s, still somewhat craft-oriented, could easily have coped with its mass production.

It is worth quoting part of the article the Commissar in charge of the Soviet pavilion wrote in the *Courrier parisien*:

Is it surprising that the Soviet pavilion has created a sensation? Among all the bourgeois suites of drawing-room and dining-room furniture the two inscriptions 'Workers' Club' and 'Village Reading-Room' (*Izba chitalnaya*) strike a note of revolutionary protest against luxury. At present everyone in Paris knows the word *izba*. It appears in every newspaper. . . . Rodchenko's work, the club, has attracted considerable attention.

After the exhibition the Soviet state presented the whole of the *Workers' Club* installation to the French Communist Party.

Rodchenko took part in the Paris exhibition primarily as an artist, but he was also involved in its organization. He went to Paris in March 1925 and spent three and a half months there. This was the artist's first and only journey abroad.[34]

In the graphic design section of the exhibition Rodchenko presented his photomontage illustrations for Mayakovsky's *About This.* In the section called 'the art of the street' he exhibited posters with Mayakovsky texts; the theatrical section included his models and scenery designs; the furniture section his *Workers' Club.* The judging committee of the Paris exhibition awarded Rodchenko four silver medals.

Paris aroused complex feelings in Rodchenko. Impressed as he was by the technical achievements of the French and by the quality and abundance of merchandise he saw, he felt depressed by the bourgeois way of life he witnessed there. The letters he sent home, parts of which appeared in the first number of *Novii Lef* in 1927, reflect his state of mind. They supply information on the exhibition as well as on the artist's work in furnishing the Soviet pavilion:

Yesterday, while watching some people foxtrotting, I wished I were in the East instead of the West. But it is in the West we have to learn organization; in the East we have to work. . . .

They say there is a Russian café here, where the atmosphere is unbearable. They sing Russian songs and actually weep with grief. They say that those unable to return to the Soviet Union find it almost impossible to endure their fate. I am sure, if I were told that I was not to return, I should sit down in the middle of the road and burst into tears. . . .

The fall of Europe . . . no, Europe is not finished. All that Europe created can still be made use of, it only has to be washed, cleaned, and set to some purpose.

The pavilion has been painted according to my plans, red, grey and white; it is a success, but nobody has said a single word about my having had anything to do with it, although everyone runs to me for advice.

The colour scheme of the Grand Palais, six halls, is also my work, and again they keep silent about it.

Polyakov and I arranged the following halls: (1) handicraft objects; (2) Vkhutemas; (3) graphic art, advertising and architecture; (4) porcelain and glass; (5) textiles. The village reading-room, and probably the theatre auditorium, are still to follow.

I went to see the Salon des Indépendants. What insignificance and lack of talent! The French seem to have run out of breath. Thousands of canvases of no consequence; simply provincial; really, this is not what I had expected. After Picasso, Braque and Léger there is indeed nothing but a vacuum. . . .

The objects surrounding us should be our equals and companions, not black, dull robot machines like these here. . . .

There are millions of objects here, they make one giddy; it would be good to buy up and send things home by the ton. They produce so many different articles that one feels poor for not being able to buy them all. . . . Now I understand the capitalist for whom nothing is enough, for objects are the opium of life. One is either a Communist or a capitalist. There is no third way.

Films and the theatre

Films and the theatre were channels through which the heroic but still unrealizable plans of the Constructivists could be realized. The young republic was too poor and unprepared for Tatlin's tower or Lavinsky's 'city suspended in the air', and even for the materialization of the more modest Constructivist conceptions and plans. This is one reason, if not the most important one, that the Constructivists liked to work for the theatre. A contemporary artist aptly remarked that 'the theatre made it possible for Constructivism to be materialized in large forms and to thus come into closer rapport with man'. Popova, Vesnin, Tatlin, Stepanova, Malevich, Rodchenko, Gan, Yakulov, the Stenberg brothers, and Medunetsky all contributed to the development of the Soviet Constructivist theatre of the 1920s.

During the period following the Revolution, Rodchenko's first stage designs were connected with 'the theatre for the masses': In 1920 he designed a series of seventeen costumes for Alexei Gan's play We [151]. These strictly geometrical sketches of indistinct colours still followed the easel-painting approach, unlike his later works in which, availing himself of the possibilities offered by the theatre, Rodchenko brought his work in the applied arts into closer rapport with man, designing 'true' clothes and furniture.

Rodchenko contributed to the periodical Kino-Fot mainly as an artist, but he had stronger ties with the actual film world. From 1922 onwards he cooperated with the film director Dziga Vertov in shooting a newsreel series originally called Kino-Pravda and later called One-sixth of the World. In addition to designing film posters and advertisements, he worked on the development of a new type of caption. It was he who made the first photomontage poster and the cover of the programme for Eisenstein's film *The Battleship Potemkin* [156–57].

In the second half of the 1920s Rodchenko's associations with film became even closer and more extensive [152–57]. Between 1927 and 1930 he took part as 'constructor-artist' in the production of the films *The Woman Journalist* (directed by Kuleshov), *Moscow in October* (directed by Barnet), *Albidum* (directed by Obolensky), *The Puppet Millionaire* (directed by Komarov), and *What shall I be?* (directed by Zhemchuzhny). With the documentary film *The Chemicalization of the Forest* Rodchenko also tried his hand at directing.

The artist was mainly attracted by films in which the material aspect of people's ways of life played an important part. These films provided Rodchenko with an excellent opportunity for the material realization of his furniture and clothing designs as well as for the propagation of the new way of life. The films entitled *Albidum*, for which Rodchenko designed a hunting-lodge, a stock exchange, a ballroom, and a study, and *Woman Journalist*, for which he furnished an editorial office, built a pavilion, and designed furniture and costumes, were films of this type. Beside being simple, economical and functional, Rodchenko's suites of furniture were highly aesthetic. Due to the economic situation of the country, Rodchenko worked in wood, as before, in spite of the fact that he had already successfully experimented with other materials (such as metal tubes).

Of course Rodchenko's interest in films and the theatre was not confined to their role as a channel for his artistic energy or as a medium through which he could popularize the models he had designed for objects of everyday use. Here too, as in other fields of work, he emerged as a creative artist who interpreted the artist's vocation in a broad and objective sense. He was a designer who thought in aesthetic terms, and a personality who would not tolerate banality or conformity. Rodchenko was never content with the role of a passive stage designer. He was convinced that the artist ought to have a say in every detail of the creative process, contributing to the development of the action, and ensuring that, instead of being a mere background setting, the material surroundings would actively participate in the film or in the theatrical scenes:

The artist must find characteristic objects for the film that haven't yet become commonplace, and he must present familiar objects, where possible, from a new angle. ... I believe that the artist's task in the production of a film is not confined to that of a decorator. He should take an interest in everything and assist in the production wherever he can. Objects without a function have no place in a film, as films do not tolerate the kind of naturalism associated with a 'life-like' outlook. Owing to the shortness of visual impressions, certain effects must be amplified, while others, just to the contrary, must be neutralized. (*Sovietskoe Kino*, 1927, No. 5–6.)

For Rodchenko 1929 was the year of the theatre. He took part in the production of two plays: Glebov's *Pendulum* at the Moscow Revolutionary Theatre [159–65] and Mayakovsky's satire, *The Bed Bug*, at the Meyerhold Theatre [158, 166].

Rodchenko designed the costumes and props for *Pendulum*: 'The constructor-artist, A. M. Rodchenko, has embarked upon an interesting experiment,' remarked *Pravda* in its issue of 28 March 1928. 'Some of his objects are extremely original and could indeed be used in everyday life. He is trying out new styles in costumes as well.'

The Bed Bug, a 'festive comedy', was a satire on surviving pre-Revolutionary habits. Mayakovsky explained:

The issue is the exposure of the petty bourgeois of today. ... In my play the hero ignominiously renounces his class for selfish interests. ... His politics are the consequence of his petty-bourgeois attitudes in everyday life.

It was twelve years since the Revolution, and the tender shoots of a Socialist culture were springing up everywhere; but Mayakovsky saw weeds sprouting as well, for the bourgeois life-style and attitudes had struck deep roots in homes, in institutions and in the dark recesses of the human soul. The theme was not a new one for Mayakovsky, but his satire in this play is more unrelenting than ever.

At Mayakovsky's suggestion the young Kukrinsky brothers and Rodchenko were invited to take part in the production of the play. The costumes for the first part, set in 1929, were designed by the Kukrinskys, while the costumes and props for the second part, supposed to take place in 1979, were the work of Rodchenko. These were symbolic, or 'poster-like' as Rodchenko put it, and reflected the artist's wit and inexhaustible ingenuity. Bearing in mind the character of the play, Rodchenko did not insist on realistic furniture for the interior, but neither did he design futuristic furniture. Instead he designed light, easily convertible structures, developing them in the Constructivist traditions of the early 1920s [158]. He designed every piece of the stage furniture to contrast with the material world of the petty-bourgeois. The critics commented favourably on the artist's work, but its most valuable recognition came from Mayakovsky himself, who gave him a printed copy of the play inscribed: 'To dear Rodchenko, from Co-author Vladimir.'

Rodchenko's next and last theatrical season was in 1931. That year he designed costumes and props for the performance of *One-sixth of the World* and *Army of Peace*, produced at the Revue and Zavadsky Theatres respectively. On 12 March 1931 the paper *Sovietskoe Iskusstvo* (*Soviet Art*) had this to say on the subject:

The work of the constructor-artist should be especially appreciated. It is that of a personality who should have been drawn into work of the Revue Theatre long ago. There are no painted rags, no adornments – the whole construction is simple, witty and to the point, and enables all sorts of conversions for quick scene-shifting.

167 *Portrait of Rodchenko* 1938

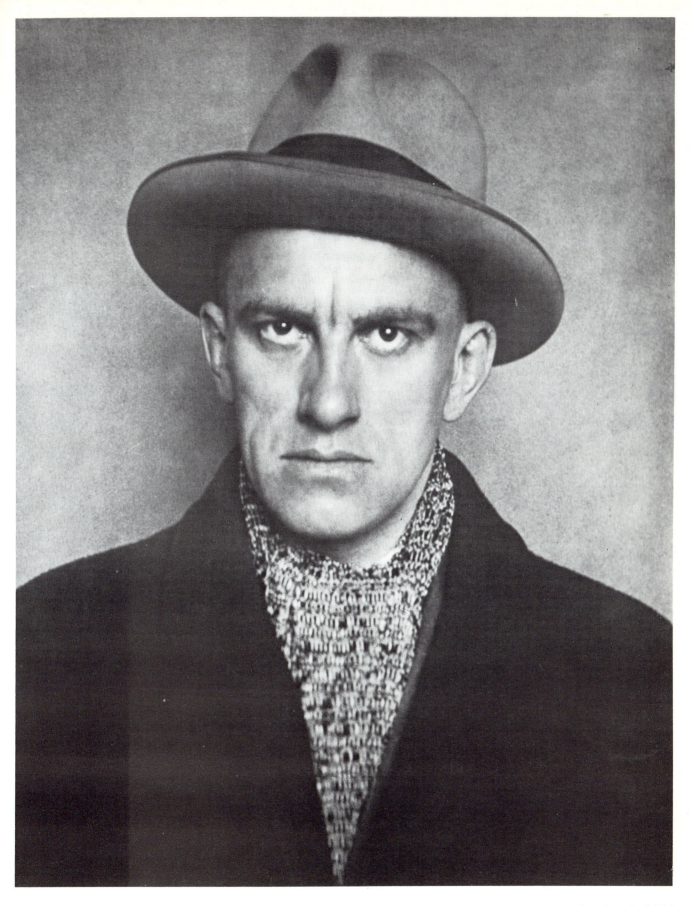

168 *Mayakovsky with his Dog* 1926   169 *Vladimir Mayakovsky* 1924

170 *Portrait of the Poet Nikolai Aseyev* 1927   171 *Spruce-firs at Pushkino* 1927

172 *Portrait of the Film Director Alexander Dovzhenko* 1930

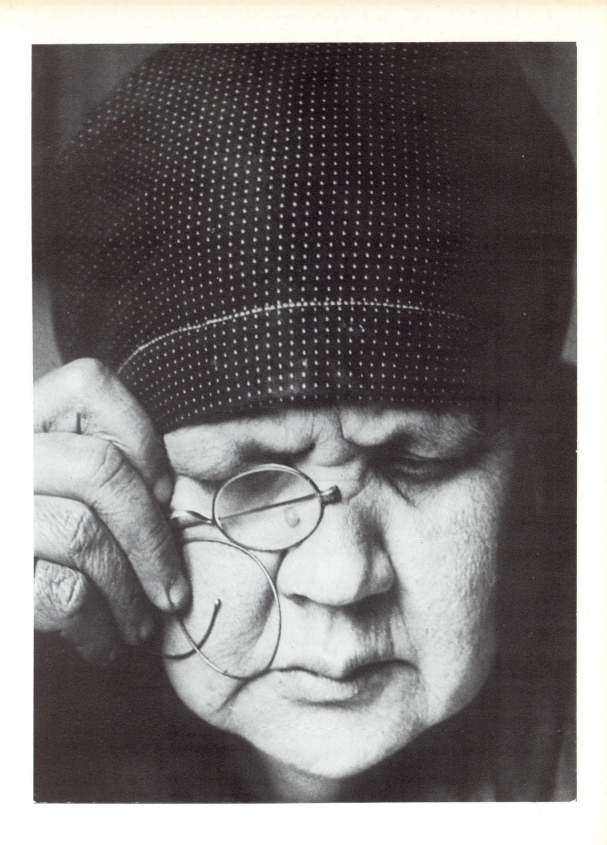

173 *The Artist's Mother* 1924

174 *Courtyard with Trees* 1927   175 *Courtyard in Myasnytskaya Street* 1927

176 *On the Fire-escape* 1927   177 *Street* 1927

178 *Glass and Light* 1928

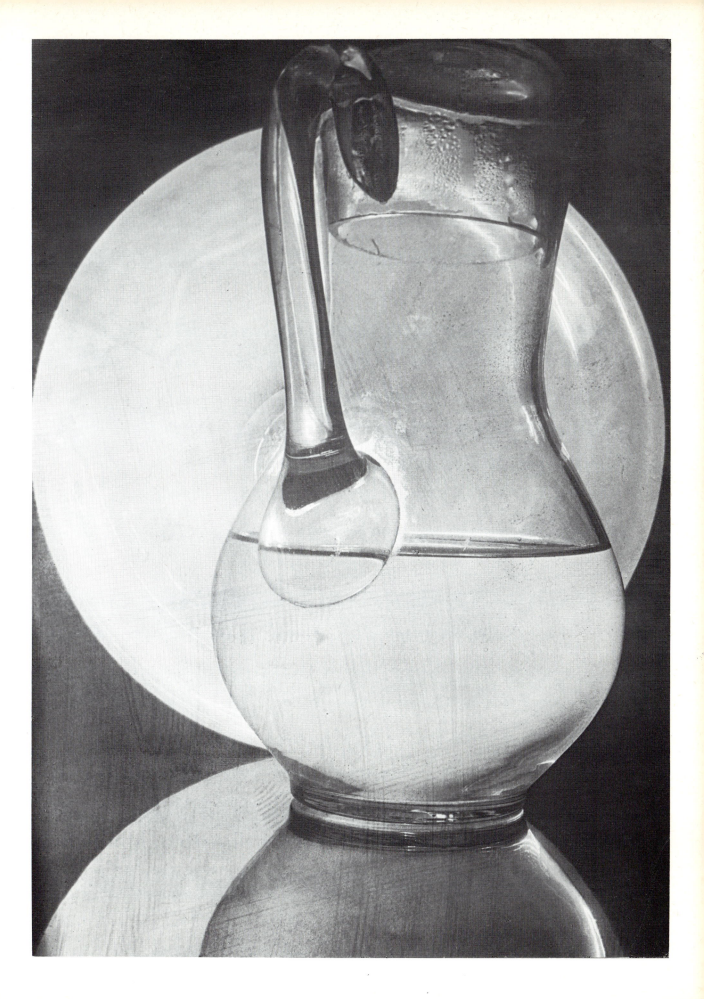

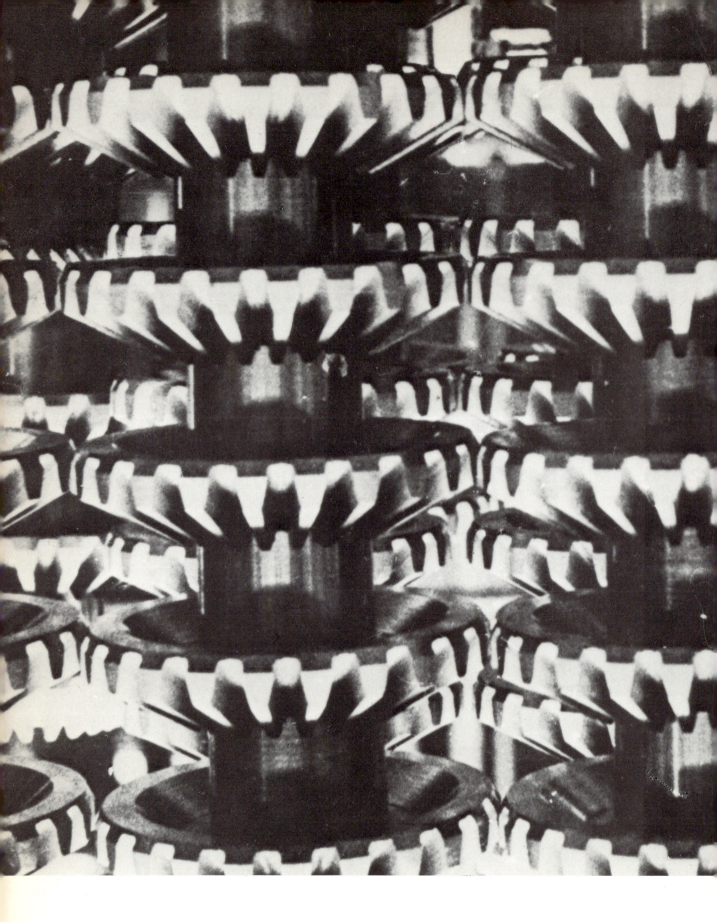

180 *Cog-wheels* 1930

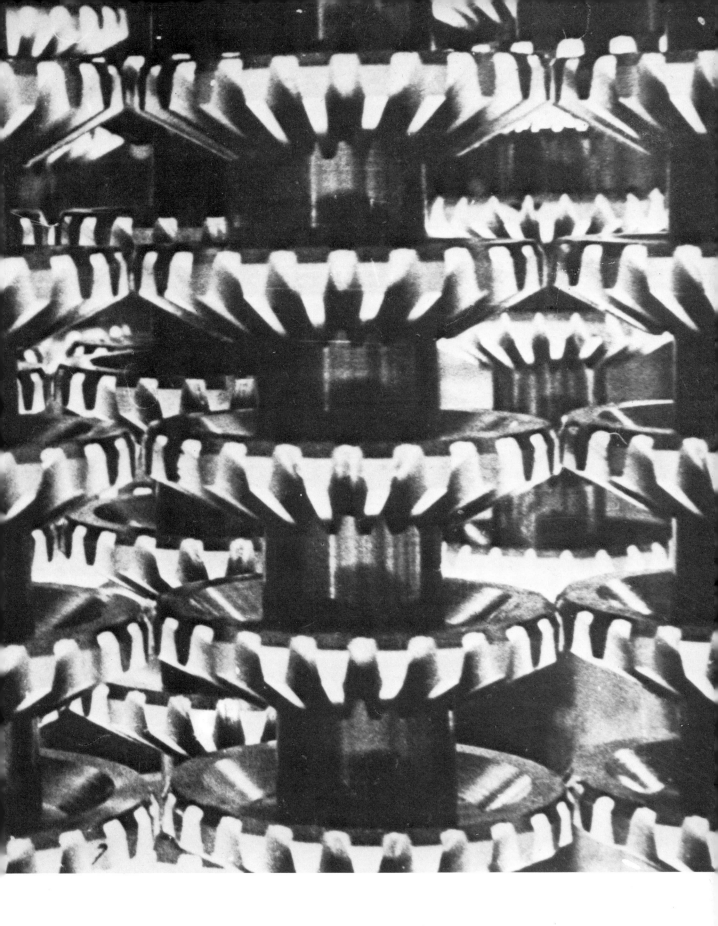

181 *Cog-wheels* 1930

213

186 *Barge at the Lock* 1933
187 *Pioneer Girl* 1930

188 *Make Way for the Women* 1935

189 *Pole-vault* 1937
190 *Free-style Diver* 1936
191 *Free-style Diver* 1936

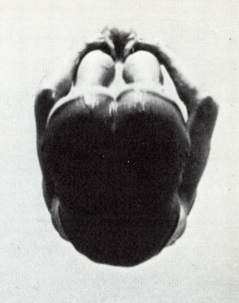

192 *Wild Flowers (The Artist's Daughter)* 1937

Master of modern photography

'The object-lens of the camera is the eye of the cultural man of socialist society. (A. M. Rodchenko.)

Rodchenko's work in the field of photography deserves a book to itself.[35] He was one of the founders of modern Soviet photographic art, and one of its most individual representatives, introducing into it an inventive spirit that found its outlet in bold experiments. His single pictures and impressive narrative series breathed fresh air, conveying the intense rhythm of the Soviet people's everyday life, the nobility of work, and the joy of youth and health.

Rodchenko began taking photographs in 1924. He first used the camera to take pictures for his photomontages. By 1927–28 he already ranked among the professional photographic artists, although it cannot be said that he was welcome in their circles, especially the more conservative ones.

After the dissolution of the Lef group, Rodchenko joined the photo section of the October artists' union,[36] where the spirit of Productivist art, so close to him, was still alive. In 1931 he was expelled from the October group 'for propagating a taste alien to the proletariat' and 'for trying to divert proletarian art to the road of Western-style advertising, formalism and aesthetics'.

In other countries the basic tendencies in modern photography were already established by the 1920s, and founded on a well-developed technology. Their exponents included such outstanding artists as Edward Weston, Edward Steichen, Man Ray and others from whom a great deal could be learned. So Rodchenko set out to learn. This did not, however, mean that he copied other artists, for the concept of copying simply did not exist in his creative vocabulary. He learned so that he might also contribute to the development of photography as an art.

His earliest works and experiments carried him straight to the heart of the problems of modern photographic art. Endeavouring to acquire a thorough knowledge of the means of expression in photography, he experimented with various techniques, discovered technological secrets and investigated the potentials of the 'mechanical eye'.

The only doctrine he consciously submitted to in his work was that 'photography must employ its own means'. He did not resort to retouching, to the use of bromide, or to any of the cosmetic tricks that had been employed for decades with a view to raising photography to an artistic level while concealing the true features of the picture.

He experimented a great deal with double exposure, repeated copying, close-up shots, and light effects. He investigated the potential of negative pictures and of various new camera angles, [170–71, 174–77] which, as possibilities of conveying aesthetic function, immediately caught his attention. Rodchenko's experience with non-objective painting and graphic art was a great help in his efforts to learn the means of expression proper to photography. He made excellent use of his highly developed visual faculty and his refined sense of form and composition.

Rodchenko the photographer inherited his appreciation of technique from Rodchenko the Constructivist, and his respect for facts in the broader sense of the word from Rodchenko, the member of Lef, 'What to shoot', 'how', 'for what purpose', were the principles that guided him in his work. He remarked in 1928:

A fetishistic attitude towards facts is not only unnecessary but even harmful in photography. We have to find – and, since we are searching, don't worry, we *shall* find – the new aesthetic, the new impulse and emotion suitable for expressing the new Soviet facts by photographic means in the language of art. The picture of a newly reconstructed factory will not simply represent a building, but will convey the pleasure and pride we feel in the industrialization of the Soviet Union, and we have to find the way to express this. It is our duty to experiment.

Rodchenko's name figures in the history of photographic art first of all because of his excellent photo-reportages and series of photographs centred on special subjects. But he also contributed many valuable works to other branches of photography. In portrait photography, for example, he proved a keen observer and a good psychologist. One of the most characteristic features of his works in this field is that in addition to the subject of the portrait one feels the presence of a second person, the artist. A peculiar atmosphere of mutual trust emanates from these pictures. The model transfers his confidence in the artist to the lens: he does not hold himself aloof, but is relaxed enough to present the image he himself has formed of his own personality. It was by giving the model this chance for self-expression that Rodchenko created the majority of the photographic portraits of his friends and comrades [168–70, 172], among them the famous Mayakovsky series. The pictures he took of members of his family are more personal and lyrical [172, 192].

Rodchenko experimented successfully with close-up photography and with shots of transparent objects placed in front of a source of light. The lens of his camera discovered objects of unusual architecture, rhythm and plasticity in cog-wheels removed from their usual surroundings, or in a bundle of newspapers [180–81]. The viewer who sees only a study in the picture of the glass jug illuminated from behind, fails to appreciate the masterly composition, the noble purity of the lines, the rich plasticity of the form and consequently also the poetry and beauty of the picture, and still more important, its specifically photographic qualities [178–79]. Rodchenko's photos are free from any components that lack a functional role.

Rodchenko attained outstanding results in photo-journalism. He was already experimenting in this field in 1924. His first reportage, entitled *Where Money is Made* and published in the periodical *Tekhnika i Zhizn* (*Technique and Life*), was a report on the workers and working processes at the Goznak Office.[37] But the time was not ripe for true photo-reporting until 1926 or 1927 when simple, portable Leica cameras were mass-produced. Armed with his Leica, Rodchenko soon conquered almost every Moscow periodical. He worked as photo-reporter for the magazines *Ogonok, Radioslushatel, Prozhektor, Krasnoye Studenchestvo, Dayosh, Za rubezhom, Smena, Borba klassov*[38] and the daily *Vechernaya Moskva*, among others. In the 1927 exhibition in commemoration of the tenth anniversary of the Revolution, and in that of 1928 entitled 'Ten Years of Soviet Photographic Art', Rodchenko participated as a photographer. At the former exhibition he put four of his photographs on show, including the one entitled *Courtyard in Myasnitskaya Street* [175]. At the latter he exhibited six works.

Although the jury of the 1928 exhibition awarded Rodchenko an honourable mention, this marked the beginning of the artist's long and exhausting struggle against his adversaries, the conservative critics and artist-photographers. Fighting for the right to experiment and for a photography free of naturalism and false romanticism, he learned both the joy of victory and the bitterness of defeat. Others copied him, learned from his work, yet rejected him; he was both glorified and persecuted, recognized and passed over in utter silence; one day he was set on a pedestal, only to be put before the public tribunal on the next, and forced to repent such alleged sins as formalism, aestheticism and slavish imitation of the West. It is almost unbelievable that these criticisms of his works were made in earnest.

In 1931–32 Rodchenko switched from reporting for periodicals to the photographic elaboration of different subjects in long series of pictures collected in albums and picture books. The artist's favourite themes in the 1930s were sports, the circus and festive processions [183, 189–91], although he successfully covered other topics as well. Between 1933 and 1941 he compiled ten extra issues for the periodical entitled *The Soviet Union in Construction*, including *The White Sea Canal* (1933); *Kazakhstan* (1935); *Parachutists* (1935); *The Russian Forest* (1936); *Soviet Gold* (1937); *The Moscow-Volga Canal* (1938); *VSHV* (National Agricultural Exhibition, 1939); *Twenty years of Goelro* (1941).[39] The photogravure entitled *The White Sea Canal* was the result of strenuous work for three months on the construction site. The two thousand negatives show men at work and resting, the outlines of the gigantic construction as it gradually takes shape, pictures of the bleak and virgin landscape of the north, and scenes bearing the marks of man's efforts to alter Nature. Rodchenko presented what he saw impartially, without interpretation, idealization or superfluous dramatization. Working conditions were extremely hard and the techniques employed were primitive, yet man was ultimately triumphant.

It was the experience of this triumph that inspired Rodchenko's impressive composition *Barges in the Lock* [186]. To enhance the panoramic effect of this picture, the artist used photomontage in such a way that the left side is repeated on the right, like a mirror-image. To modify the symmetry, he touched out three human figures from one side. *The Russian Forest*, which he made in 1936 for No. 8 of the periodical *The Soviet Union in Construction*, is another of Rodchenko's impressive works. The potentially prosaic theme – a report on the work of the Soviet timber exporting companies – was developed into a poetic and even philosophical series of pictures of man and Nature, and their organic relationship. The excellent quality of the photographs, their depth, the arrangement of the material and the completeness of the total conception justify us in evaluating this work as a masterpiece of photographic art. Rodchenko's work did not remain unnoticed.

No publication comparable to this number of the periodical has ever been made on the timber trade before. . . . The Soviet Union has achieved good results not only in the field of industry. . . . If they can pride themselves on their timber trade, they are at least as much entitled to take pride in their results in the fields of photography, arrangement of the material and typography.

This quotation is from the British weekly *The Timber Trades Journal*, which in September 1936 published a review of *The Soviet Union in Construction*.

In the second half of the 1930s Rodchenko and Varvara Stepanova jointly produced a series of photo-albums and picture books to celebrate the anniversary of the Soviet Union. In the preparation of *The First Cavalry Troop* (1935–37), an impressive historical album, Rodchenko acted as designer, photographer and leader of the reporters' photo group. Other works of these years include the albums entitled *The Red Army* (1938), *The Soviet Air Force* and *Marching Youth.* The latter figured at the 1939 New York World's Fair.

In 1940, to commemorate the tenth anniversary of Mayakovsky's death, Rodchenko designed the volume which was to contain the selected works of the poet. At the same time he and Stepanova jointly produced No. 7 of the periodical *The Soviet Union in Construction*, devoted to Mayakovsky's work. At an exhibition of Mayakovsky's *oeuvre* a whole room was allocated to Rodchenko's photographic illustrations to the poem *Vladimir Ilyich Lenin* and to his large mural montage *Lenin and the Party*.

193 Rodchenko with his daughter Varvara Alexandrovna 1948

194 *Circus Rider* 1935   195 *Romance* 1935

196 *Middle Ages* 1940
197 *Gravity* 1940

198 *Masked Woman* 1941
199 *The Fastidious Woman* 1946

200 *Profiles* 1948

234

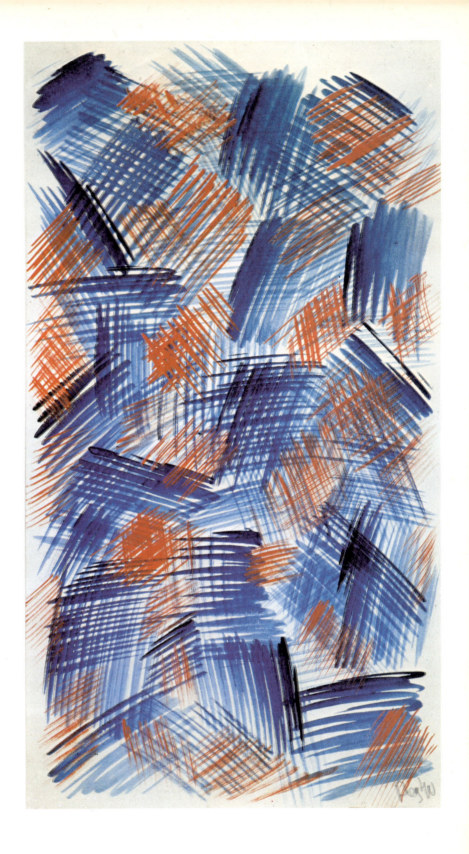

201 *Textile Design* 1940

202 *Composition* 1940

203 *Composition* 1940

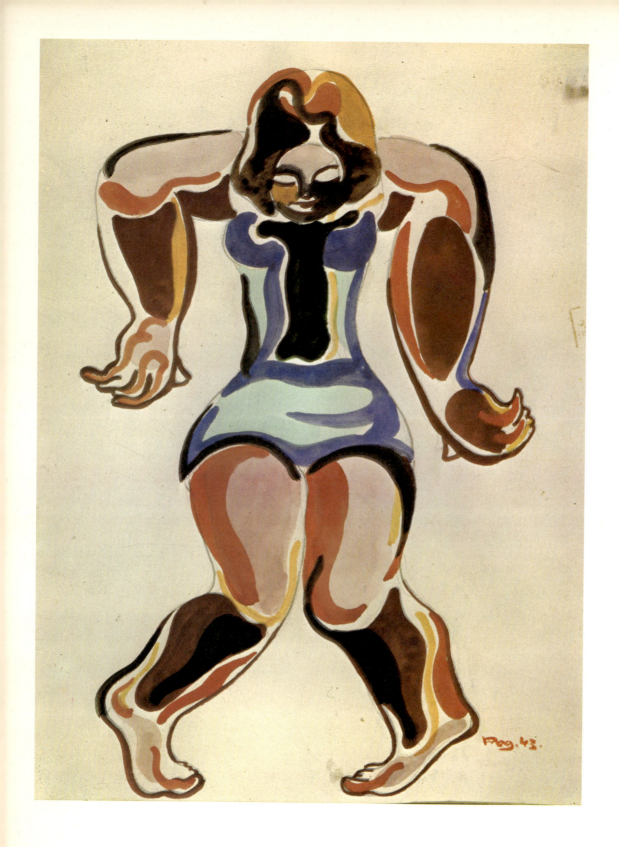

Poq.43.

205 *Masks* 1943

206 *Composition* 1944

207 *Composition* 1941
208 *Composition* 1941

209 *Composition* 1941

243

210 *Composition* 1941

211 Rodchenko at his easel 1948

Rodchenko's photography: writings by the artist and critics

One falters in front of an object, building or man, wondering how best to photograph it — this way or that way or which way? Everyone knows this, for we have been trained for thousands of years to see things according to the rules of composition of our elders' time. But man must be revolutionized, so that he can see the objects from different angles and in any light. *Soviet Foto* asked me to contribute to the periodical. I went to see the editors and asked whether I owed this invitation to their having seen Moholy-Nagy's book.[40] 'Yes,' they replied. 'We even gave it publicity once, but then we realized that we had Leftist artists of our own.' From among my works *Soviet Foto* prefers those which have appeared on *Lef*. When I take them new ones they do not say a word. God knows what is good and what is bad. It is a new thing, difficult to understand.

(Rodchenko, *Novii Lef*, No. 6, 1927.)

The most interesting visual angles of our age are the bird's eye view and the worm's eye view, and we have to adopt them in our work. I do not know who discovered them, but I suppose they have been in existence for a long time. All I have to do is to improve their application and get them accepted.

(Rodchenko, *Novii Lef*, No. 5, 1928.)

There was an article in the periodical *Soviet Foto* written with the intention of bringing discredit to my authority and discouraging the photo-artists from working in new perspectives.

(Rodchenko, *Novii Lef*, No. 9, 1928.)

A. M. Rodchenko is an original artist whose work strikes a new and completely individual note, which makes his creations different from those of all other artists. He has several epigones who follow his belief and often even copy him blindly. Every piece of work of this interesting artist inspires thoughts and develops our aesthetic perceptions.

(*Fotograf*, No. 5, 1929.)

Why is the Pioneer girl [187] shown looking upwards? It is ideologically wrong. Pioneers and Komsomolists should look forward.

(A member of the jury of the 1935 photographic exhibition.)

I have stopped rebelling and trying to be original; I am no longer rash in shooting my photos; I no longer photograph in perspective for perspective's sake, nor from bird's eye view, whether it is necessary or not. I work on the contents, rather than on the appearance of the pictures.

(Rodchenko, 1935.)

Rodchenko's work is of tremendous significance; few photo-reporters have been able to escape his influence, even those who held decidedly opposite views.

(From the catalogue of the exhibition 'Masters of Photographic Art', 1935.)

The title of the exhibition: 'Masters of Photographic Art' is applicable first and foremost to Rodchenko.

(*Soviet Foto*, No. 7, 1935.)

In the photo entitled *The Soviet Swimming Instructor* the viewer would like to see a well built, athletic body. In A. Rodchenko's picture the figure is smothered by naturalistic details. The photograph clearly proves that formalist practice is not free from naturalism either.

(*Soviet Foto*, Nos. 5–6, 1936.)

It is not easy to speak when one's whole life-work is being called in question. And who should be the first to question it, but the artist himself. This is a difficult problem, painful to talk about, for one not only has to judge works that required a tremendous creative effort, but also to explain their contents, technique and method. Every piece of my work was created in the spirit of the attitude to life that I had fought for, and with every one I aimed at a high standard of technical skill.

(Rodchenko's self-criticism at an art debate in 1936, announced under the slogan 'Against formalism and naturalism'.)

We must publish truly high quality artistic photos and reports, and devote space to the examples of experimental photography.

(Rodchenko, 'What the periodical *Soviet Foto* should be like', *Soviet Foto*, No. 9, 1937)

The Jury decided to award the First Class Diploma to Comrade Rodchenko for the high artistic level of his exhibited works showing an international mass sports festival.

(Resolution of the jury of the First Federal Exhibition of Photo Art)

Among Rodchenko's excellent material, one picture met with general incomprehension on the part of the visitors. . . . For the sake of formal composition the artist presented two patches of balancing tones by deliberately bending the head of the girl sitting at the table in front of a bunch of flowers [1927]. This photo must have gained admittance to the exhibition only thanks to the exaggerated liberalism of the Jury.

(*Soviet Foto*, No. 3, 1938, on the photo entitled *Wild Flowers*)

Rodchenko on the artistic potential of photography

It is almost impossible to overlook how hard we endeavour to discover all the potentialities of photography.

As in a marvellous fairy tale or dream, we discover the miracles of photography in their amazing reality.

Applied photography imitating etchings, paintings, or carpets, is following new paths of its own; it flourishes and emanates a characteristic scent. Possibilities never before seen lie open before it.

The numerous planes of images with finely traced outlines surpass the effects of photomontage. There are transitions from the complete whole to the finest tiny veins.

The contrasts of perspective. Light contrasts. Contrasts of forms. View-points inaccessible to drawing or painting. Foreshortening with strong distortion of the photographed object and the rough texture of the material.

Perfectly new, unprecedented representation of movement by man, animal, machine, etc. Moments we didn't know of or, if we did, couldn't see, like the flight of a bullet, for example.

Compositions whose boldness surpasses the imagination of the painter; a formal wealth that leaves Rubens' works far behind.

Compositions with an extremely complex play of lines, which the Dutch and the Japanese cannot approach.

Then there is also the creation of non-existent moments by the use of montage on a photo.

The negative picture conveys totally new stimulations to the senses.

Not to mention the double exposure (in film: dissolving), optical distortions, the photography of reflections, and similar possibilities.

The photographers have shown themselves to be masters with individual taste, style and manner. They continue working on their subjects and style with perseverance.

Photographic art is developing rapidly, conquering more and more ground. ... Its development matches the advances witnessed in painting.

Technically, photography is simple and quick; it has become such an indispensable requisite of science, life and technology, and a thing within such easy reach, that it is still not considered able to act as its own prophet ... nor is its right to its own creative artists recognized.

The love of photography must be fostered until people begin to collect photographs. (Photo collections and immense photo exhibitions must be assembled.)

Instead of so-called 'salons', international photo exhibitions should be organized.

Periodicals and books on photography must be published.

Photography has every right and every merit to claim our attention as the art of our age.

(Rodchenko, 1934)

Black and white

. . . Then he began to photograph.
In his hands the nickel and glass black Leica
went to work with joy.
Now he'll reveal the world.
From a new viewpoint
the familiar and everyday world.
He'll reveal the people and the building of Socialism
more potently and exaltedly.
Now he'll agitate with photography.
For everything young, new and original.
But here . . . the flight was cut off.
Once again the red lamp shines on the stage.
The auditorium is dark and empty.
No flight. . . .
No applause. . . .
The critics attack him with all their strength.
On account of the formalism, the foreshortenings, and other things.
He became a lonely child again.
They considered him harmful and dangerous.
They imitated him, but they turned away from him.
The friends were afraid even to visit him.
And he decided to withdraw. . . .
From the stage of photography, disillusioned and weary.

Does the land of Socialism have no need
for ventriloquists,
magicians and jongleurs?
For fireworks, planetariums, flowers,
kaleidoscopes? . . .
Exhausted he prepared for the exhibition
of Soviet master photographers.
He didn't even know what to exhibit.
They'll only judge him over again.
He would ponder: is it worth it to take part?
In the end, he decided to do it.
And suddenly — success!
It came, Ovations.
He took off and began to soar. . . .
The endless possibilities of creation
opened up before him once again.
The auditorium filled up with friends and acquaintances.
They demand.
They demand experiments and fantasies
from the little boy. Everything he had ever dreamt of. . . .

(Rodchenko, 1939. From his autobiography.)

1941–1956: a brief chronology

In the winter of 1941 Rodchenko and his family were evacuated. The artist worked at the Ochera branch of the Molotov Fine Arts Federation and for the paper *Stalinsky Udarnik* (*Stalin Superworker*). For a short time he also contributed to *Stalinskaya Putyovka* (*Stalin Pass*) which again offered him an opportunity to resume photography.

In the summer of 1942 Rodchenko returned to Moscow where he was entrusted with the mounting of exhibitions for Sovinformburo.

In 1943 he took part in the organization of the photo exhibition 'The History of the Party', staged in the Museum of the Revolution.

In 1944–45 he was the artistic director of House of Technique.

In 1945–48, together with Stepanova, he edited the silver jubilee album *25 years of the Kazakh Soviet Republic*, and *Thirty Years of Soviet Literature*.

In 1949, together with Stepanova, he worked on a series of posters devoted to Mayakovsky. He also embarked on an entry for a Bolshoi Theatre competition to design sets for the ballet *Sleeping Beauty*, but illness prevented him from completing his plans.

In 1953 Rodchenko was engaged in designing a series of posters covering the subject of agricultural work.

In 1955 he contributed two portraits of Mayakovsky to a photo exhibition at the House of Journalists.

In 1956 Rodchenko and Stepanova worked on Mayakovsky's book *Marvellous!*

Back to art

Perhaps a more suitable title for this section would be 'Back to easel painting', for Rodchenko was never unfaithful to art or his vocation of artist. It is true that in the course of his artistic Odyssey he sometimes came near the border, but thanks to his artistic instinct he never actually crossed it. The epithets 'militant functionalist', 'negator of aesthetic qualities' and 'apostle of the philosophy of useful objects' have become practically inseparable from the names of Rodchenko and his associates. In the eyes of some of their contemporaries the resolution of the group to seek creative ground in productive work appeared to be artistic suicide. This view was, however, mistaken. Although the Productivists rejected 'pure art', they remained artists: the artists of the theatre, films, books, posters, furniture, fashion, etc. They never intended to become tailors, carpenters or technicians, nor did they aspire to replace engineers and constructors when they participated as constructor-artists in the productive process.

In the mid 1930s Rodchenko resumed easel painting. As to the reasons which induced him to take up brush, pen and pencil again, we have to content ourselves with educated guesses at best. After the dissolution of Vkhutein, Rodchenko was obliged to give up teaching, a profession to which he had attached great value. Owing to the discredit brought upon his creative principles, and to the well-known events that took place in the country's cultural life in the early 1930s, he also had to give up his activities in other fields where his many-sided talent had flourished.

Having been constantly involved with the most varied branches of art, this change was particularly hard on him. All that remained for him was photography and the few threads that tied him to book design; but self-expression in these fields was also confined within strict limits. Rodchenko continued to perform his work with honest devotion, but the scope he was granted proved too narrow for him: not that he was condemned to inactivity even for a moment, for he always had plenty to do – in fact, he was overburdened with tasks – but the burden was a physical one. Intellectually he was practically starved, a condition which produced a steadily growing emotional tension. It was in order to ease this tension and to abandon himself to his thoughts that he took up the brush and began painting again. He did not paint for commissions or for exhibitions, but for his own pleasure. He painted with his old enthusiasm, passion and creative power.

In 1935 Rodchenko started work on a series of pictures of his favourite subject: the circus. In some of these works the artist's yearning for colour put every shade of the rainbow on his palette, to evoke the magical atmosphere of his subject. But as soon as he assuaged his craving for colours he switched to a more restrained grey tonality. The drawing is of a noble simplicity throughout; the forms are united and powerful. The figures in the series are acrobats, circus riders and clowns; people with whom Rodchenko especially sympathized. The pictures form a series by virtue of their general subject matter, rather than of their contents [194].

In addition to the pictures depicting circus life, mention should be made of those in which the circus serves only as a background to the expression of the artist's emotions. His clowns – most of whom are shown playing an instrument – are pensive, sad and ironical. In his painting entitled *Romance* the feeling of sorrow, and perhaps even bitterness, is strongly suggested, both in spite of and because of the bright colour [195]. The clown's face and posture, especially the curve of his shoulders and head and the gesture of his arms, express dramatic sadness. His emotions spread to the trained dog, whose knowing glance has nothing comic in it, just as there is nothing comic in the music – a romance – played by the clown.

This sad atmosphere and the pessimistic overtones are new traits in Rodchenko's art, hard to reconcile with his earlier activity. All he had created in the preceding twenty years; the drawings from his student years, the Cubo-Futurist and abstract pictures, his book covers, and his works for the theatre and film, not to mention his photographs, had spoken of joy and a positive attitude to life.

Although the bitterness which burst forth from the artist in the mid 1930s eventually subsided, his interest in representational pictures conveying states of mind persisted for a long time [196–99].

Having rediscovered easel painting, Rodchenko reached his peak in this branch of art at the end of the 1930s and beginning of the 1940s, when the pages of his sketch-pads filled with abstract compositions. After a lapse of twenty years he returned to the abstract forms he knew and understood so well; to a world of 'objects' brought to life by the artist's creative will. Prompted by a deep inner necessity rather than by a compelling feeling of nostalgia, he again set out to explore unbroken ground. While turning to abstract art, he did not sink into the past; he never repeated a single one of his old conceptions, never continued or improved upon any of his earlier series. Neither did he delve again into the formal problems which had intrigued him earlier. He began a completely original series.

The most essential characteristic of his new style was a kind of overt decorativeness which distinguished these works from those he had produced before, including his Neo-Objective creations. His drawings and paintings of this period bear no trace of exhaustion; they are fresh, vigorous, refined and elaborated with virtuosity [202–03, 206–10]. There is neither tension nor sharply defined form in them. The simple motifs, derived from capriciously entwined lines, stripes and patches, reflect the great ease with which they were created. While in the past improvisation had had a relatively modest place in Rodchenko's creative method, almost half of the motifs in his abstract works of the 1940s are the results of free improvisation. A change in the colours he now used is also striking: green and yellow grew more dominant, while black — formerly a permanent constituent of his pictures — diminished to a minimum.

These factors constitute the difference between Rodchenko's early and late abstract painting. Nevertheless, many important elements remained the same. Rodchenko changed neither his conception of abstract art as such, nor his views as to where the possible limits in the world of abstract forms lay. The incorrigible formalist, the outstanding master of purist painting, remained consistently true to the principle of pure abstract art. This fidelity persisted in spite of the fact that at the end of the 1930s he simultaneously showed a lively interest in the representation of the intricate phenomena of man's emotional life.

Among the abstract works Rodchenko created in the 1940s, there are some which, although they can hardly be placed within a single series, are stylistically related to each other. Under more favourable circumstances Rodchenko might have developed them into new series, or might have ripened his style into one of a significance beyond decoration.

Alexander Rodchenko was an artist endowed with a talent of many facets. He was an untiring explorer of new continents in the world of art and a hard worker who accomplished both small and large tasks with the utmost concentration of intellectual and physical abilities. He was one of the Russian artists who — to quote his own words from the article on Tatlin — 'created for years without any recognition, and worked until death, with great zeal and simple, pure taste, for an unknown future'.

Rodchenko died on 3 December 1956. As to the 'unknown future', its outlines are slowly but inevitably blending with those of the present day.

Notes

1 The Old Believers (*Starovery*): the successors of those who were loath to accept Patriarch Nikon's seventeenth-century reform of the prayer-books and services of the Russian Orthodox Church.

2 Leftists, Left wing: expressions widely used in Russia by critics and in artistic circles after the 1905 Revolution. They denote the radical young artists, and are actually synonyms for the avant-garde.

3 Youth Association (*Soyuz Molodiozhi*): a society of artists formed in St Petersburg in 1910. Its members, Filonov, Fonvizin, Rosanova, Malevich, Larionov, Goncharova, Tatlin, David and Vladimir Burliuk, Shkolnik, Spandikov and others, came from the young radical artists of St Petersburg and Moscow. Between 1910 and 1914 the Youth Association published a magazine of the same name, staged exhibitions and organized public debates on modern art. Its members maintained close connections with avant-garde poets and composers. In 1917 there was an attempt to revive its activities. The Youth Association represented an important stage in the development of the Russian avant-garde.

4 Knave of Diamonds (*Bubovnii Valet*): a group of young Moscow painters formed in 1910. It was so named to contrast the high-flown names of earlier groups, magazines, etc., such as 'World of Art', 'The Blue Rose' and 'Wreath'. Aristarkh Lentulov and Mikhail Larionov took active part in the formation of the group. However, as Larionov found the endeavours of its principal members, Lentulov, Mashkov, Konchalovsky, Kuprin, Rozhdestvensky and Falk, much too moderate, he broke with the Knave of Diamonds group after their first joint exhibition.

The art of the group was characterized above all by powerful and richly coloured paintings, whose 'seedbed' (to use Malevich's expression) was to be found in the forms of the material world, simplified and moderately 'Cubified'. Their artistic style developed under the influence of Van Gogh, Cézanne, Matisse and Picasso, Chinese and Japanese painting, and Russian icons and folk woodcuts (*lubok*). The association dissolved in 1917. A new group called the Moscow Painters was formed in 1925 with the participation of former members of Knave of Diamonds.

According to Lentulov, Knave of Diamonds was 'a group of painters working in the spirit of an overtly materialistic new art. (In the history of painting), this may be interpreted as a clash between two world outlooks: the individualist-mystic and the dynamic, crudely realistic and materialistic, which shocked and irritated contemporary conservative-liberal society. M. Lentulova, *Khudozhnik Aristarkh Lentulov* (*Aristarkh Lentulov the Painter*), Moscow, 1969, p. 32.

5 Primitivism: a style in Russian avant-garde art, represented by painters like Larionov (the initiator of the movement), Goncharova, Burliuk, and Malevich. The Russian Primitivist period lasted from 1907 to 1910. The style found its source in the naïve drawings and legends associated with inn and shop signs, in 'wall drawings' in the streets, in the folk woodcut (*lubok*) and wood carvings, in children's drawings, in medieval Russian frescoes and icons, and in Eastern art. The main characteristics of this highly expressive art were lively colouring, minimal contour lines, and ornamental articulation of the picture surface.

6 *The Garden of Judges* (*Sadok Sudei*): The circumstances of the creation of this volume are described by the Futurist poet Vassily Kamensky in his interesting autobiography: 'We were fully aware that with this book we had laid the foundations of a 'new period' of literature; we therefore decided (1) to shatter the old orthography ...; (2) to print the book on cheap wallpaper in protest against the 'de luxe' editions brought out by the bourgeoisie; (3) to make the pattern of the wallpaper the only ornament of the volume; (4) to publish only 'lyric' material, so that it should not be confiscated on the instigation of the newspapers; (5) to get Khlebnikov, David Burliuk, Nikolay Burliuk, Vassily Kamensky, Elena Guro, Myasoyedov, and E. Nyzen to write the book and Vladimir Burliuk to illustrate it with drawings; (6) the printing costs were to be covered by the authors themselves; (7) after the appearance of *The Garden of Judges* the authors were to appear in public places, read aloud from the book and proclaim the coming of the Futurists.' V. Kamensky, *Puty entuziasta* (*The Course of an Enthusiast*), Permi Publishers, 1968, p. 95.

7 *Golden Fleece* (*Zolotoe Runo*): an illustrated monthly artistic and literary review, subsidized by the prominent industrialist, patron and art collector Nikolay Ryabushinsky. It appeared in Moscow from 1906 to 1909 and became famous for its part in popularizing the latest Russian and European (mainly French) artistic trends.

It was at the initiative and with the help of *Golden Fleece* that the exhibitions entitled 'Blue Rose' (*Golubaya roza*) and 'The Wreath' (*Venok*) were staged in March 1907 and at the end of 1907, respectively, marking the birth of Russian avant-garde art. Larionov and Goncharova took active part in the work of the review.

In 1908–09 three exhibitions, considered significant events in Moscow's cultural life, were staged with the material aid of Ryabushinsky. The first was the 'Golden Fleece Salon' (April, 1908), which exhibited original works by Braque, Matisse, Derain, Van Dongen, La Fauconnier, Marquet and Vlaminck for the first time, in addition to pictures by well-known Russian artists. (The collections of Shchukin and Morosov were accessible only to few.) The second 'Golden Fleece' exhibition (January, 1909) consisted mainly of works by foreign artists. The third (late in 1909) consisted exclusively of contributions by Moscow painters.

8 *Apollo*: a fine arts periodical published in St Petersburg from 1909 to 1917. It was edited by the poet and critic Sergei Makovsky, an adherent of the ideology and aesthetic principles propagated by *Mir Iskusstva*. The periodical devoted a great deal of attention to Impressionism and Post-Impressionism, but decidedly rejected the more recent trends.

9 *Mir Iskusstva* (*World of Art*): an art and literary periodical which appeared in St Petersburg from 1899 to 1904. It was the mouthpiece of the art society functioning under the same name (see also Note 12). The paper was edited by Sergei Diaghilev, who in 1903 was joined by Alexander Benois. The literary editor was Dmitri Filosofov. Contributors included outstanding representatives of Symbolism: Merezhkovsky, Balmont, Minsky, Bely, Bryusov and Zinaida Gippius.

Mir Iskusstva spared no effort to acquaint the Russian public with French, German, British, Belgian, Finnish and Swedish art. The few exhibitions organized by Diaghilev in St Petersburg between 1897 and 1899 were also to serve this purpose. Although the Miriskusstniks had strong reservations about Impressionism and Post-Impressionism, their first exhibition (1899), which was international, included pictures by Monet, Degas and Renoir. Reproductions of pictures by Van Gogh and Cézanne appeared in their review.

The artists most appreciated by the Miriskusstniks, at least at the beginning of their career, were Puvis de Chavannes, Denis, Böcklin and Beardsley. They also continued to publicize the art of Whistler, Raffaëlli, Gallen, Edelfelt, Liebermann, Dietz and Marées. One of the 1901 issues was devoted to salon paintings. Ample space was given to the most prominent Russian artists, Vrubel, Riepin, Serov and Nestierov. From the point of view of Russian national culture, the review deserves credit for having propagated Russian classicism as rediscovered through the efforts of Benois and Diaghilev.

10 *Balance* or *Libra* (*Vesi*) : a literary and art review published in Moscow from 1904 to 1909. The most important organ of the Moscow Symbolists, it was published by Sergei Poliakov and edited by Valery Bryusov.

11 Quoted from V. Katanian, *Mayakovsky. Literaturnaya khronika* (*Mayakovsky. Literary Chronicle*), Moscow, 1961.

12 *Mir Iskusstva:* the society was founded in 1897 by Alexander Benois, Sergei Diaghilev, Dmitri Filosofov, Konstantin Somov, Lev Bakst and Yevgeni Lansere. Later Mstislav Dobuzhinsky joined. Its members upheld the principle of 'pure art' and declared war on the democratism of the Peredvizhniks on the one side, and on academism on the other. This programme determined the place of the group in Russian art life for a long time. The uncompromising battle it fought for cultured creation and for a high standard of professional skill, as well as its unprecedented advocacy of an interchange between European and Russian culture, shown in particular by Diaghilev and Benois, attracted certain artists to whom the ideological and aesthetic endeavours of the group were otherwise alien. Their exhibitions were usually important events in the cultural life of St Petersburg and Moscow. In addition to the members of the association, practically all the prominent painters in the first decades of the century contributed to these exhibitions.

Mir Iskusstva played a significant part in the rapid spread of modern trends in Russia; and yet the Miriskusstniks themselves − gifted painters, graphic artists, illustrators and stage designers though they were − manifested no special response to those trends. They had no intention of breaking either with the narrative style, or with traditional forms in their artistic practice; no trace of deformation can be found in their works. When Sergei Makovsky said that the Miriskusstniks were retrospective dreamers, he not inaptly hit on the essence of their art, although the definition was far from exhaustive. Soon after the 1903 exhibition the magazine ceased publication and the group ceased to function as a united organization.

The exhibitions were revived, with the participation of the old foundation members, by the so-called second *Mir Iskusstva* generation after 1910. The society admitted many young members, among them Serebriakova, Sapunov, Sudeikin, Narbut and Mitrohin. Petrov-Vodkin, Sarian and Boris Grigoriev also contributed to the exhibitions. With a few exceptions, the 'Leftist youth' was excluded. Benois, the ideologist of the organization, greeted the new trend gaining ground in Russian artistic life with contempt, calling it 'barbarous', 'savage' and the sign of 'spiritual destitution among the ranks of the ultra-moderns'. Diaghilev, who after 1906 threw in his lot with the Russian ballet seasons in Paris and other western European cities, showed greater flexibility in this respect. Three further *Mir Iskusstva* exhibitions were staged after the October Revolution, in 1918, 1922 and 1924.

13 Rodchenko is ranked as a Suprematist, a follower of Malevich, by Konstantin Umansky in his book *Neue Kunst in Russland, 1914–1919,* as well as by Camilla Gray in her *The Russian Experiment in Art, 1863–1922.* We are faced here with a tradition of thought whose source is easy to trace. Rodchenko's name began to be known in a comparatively wide circle of experts and regular visitors to exhibitions from 1918 onwards; that is from the time that also marked the beginning of a short Suprematist period in his art. Those who were not acquainted with the artist's earlier works or who failed to notice the qualitative changes that took place within the Suprematist movement around that time, may easily have associated Rodchenko's name with Suprematism. A number of later Soviet and other authors identified themselves with the views of the 'eye-witnesses of the events' and also uncritically classified Rodchenko as Malevich's follower. The situation is similar with a wide range of problems and facts touching upon the history of the Russian avant-garde.

14 Camilla Gray's book is one text among others which describes the controversy between Tatlin and Malevich.

15 To illustrate the misinterpretation of the essence of Russian avant-garde art we refer to Umansky's *Neue Kunst in Russland 1914–1919*. Umansky, a poet, was among the first to spread information abroad about the events in Russian artistic life during the years of the First World War. However, the picture outlined in his book was the result of rash and superficial conclusions and an extremely subjective attitude to Russian values. It is well known that he was a disciple of the 'German School', an ardent Expressionist, which explains a great deal. Under the circumstances it is comprehensible that he declared that 'Tatlinism' was not a native phenomenon in Russian art, and that in contemporary Russia 'the Spiritual in Art' triumphed in every movement, and all movements aspired after absolute Expressionism. According to Umansky, the leading role was played by Kandinsky's circle and Malevich's group (i.e. the Suprematists).

With knowledge of the true facts we may assert that this opinion is wrong. Russian avant-garde art is identical with the line of Constructivism of Larionov, Goncharova, Burliuk, Malevich and, with certain reservations, Tatlin. This line developed and grew strong by fighting what Umansky, following Kandinsky, called 'the Spiritual' – which is to say literary content, Symbolism and Expressionism – in other words, by rejecting the psychological approach in all its possible forms. The magnetic needle of the Russian avant-garde pointed first of all towards a 'healthy materialism', positivism, form, science and technology.

Many phases of Kandinsky's art had become rooted in the soil of German artistic life. Painters like Filonov and Chekrighin are unique in the history of the Russian avant-garde. Their names (the names of gifted and original creators) close the list of Expressionists whose art developed in Russia. Malevich the Suprematist and Constructivist had numerous pupils and followers, but Malevich the philosopher, who wanted to erect the 'Spiritual in Art' on Suprematist ground, is a unique phenomenon, distant from the main Russian avant-garde line.

16 Futurists: the word is used here to mean the radical group of artists and poets belonging to the Left wing of Russian art.

17 The fact that in 1917 the Knave of Diamonds group can be found in the centre of the *Mir Iskusstva* bloc, and not on the 'Leftist' side, is due to the polarization which had developed in the ranks of Russian avant-garde artists during the preceding three or four years.

18 *Zigra ar* and *Rtni khomle*: works by the Futurist poet Kruchenykh.

19 In one of the issues of *Anarchia*, a leader of the Non-Objectivists had this to say: 'Congratulations to Rozanova, the creator of dynamic compositions of lively colours! Congratulations to Udaltsova, the creator of barbarously painted Non-Objective pictures! Congratulations to Rodchenko, the creator of witty three-dimensional colour structures! Congratulations to Vesnin, the creator of black and coloured works of powerful composition! Congratulations to Drevin, the creator of bold and liberal compositions in masses of colour!' (See Bush and Zamoshkin, *Puty sovietskoy zhivopisi.1917–1933*). This issue of *Anarchia* cannot have appeared either before or after May-June 1918. The First Exhibition of the Painters' Trade Union opened around that time; it was the only joint exhibition of the enumerated artists. The style of the works they showed supports the presumption that the 'greeting' was written on the occasion of this very exhibition.

20 The members of Obmokhu (*Obshchestvo molodikh khudozhnikov*, Society of Young Artists) included many of the Vkhutemas students. The society, formed in 1919 and functioning until 1922, centred round Vladimir Stenberg, Georgy Stenberg and

Kazimir Medunetsky. Obumokhu exhibitions contained mainly three-dimensional structures, somewhat similar to Tatlin's *Counter-Reliefs* and Rodchenko's *Spatial Constructions*.

21 *Pure art* as applied here is not identical with the concept of 'art for art's sake' or *l'art pour l'art*. By pure art the Constructivists meant easel painting.

22 Quoted from: *Agitatsionno-massovoye iskusstvo pervikh let Oktyabrya* (Propagandistic Art for the Masses in the First Years after the October Revolution), Moscow, 1971, p. 129.

23 Ibid., p. 101.

24 *Vestnik iskusstv* (*Art Gazette*), 1922, No. 5. The quotation comes from a summary article entitled 'Artists' Production'.

25 Gum: state stores. Gosizdat: state publishers. Mosselprom and Rezinotorg: state owned, self-governing enterprises manufacturing and marketing light industrial goods, food and chemical products.

26 Rapp (*Rossiskaya assotsiatsiya proletarskikh pisateley* (Russian Association of Proletarian Writers) and Mapp (*Moskovskaya assotsiatsiya proletarskikh pisateley* (Moscow Association of Proletarian Writers) were literary policy-making organizations brought into being for the consolidation of proletarian literature. They committed serious ideological and political errors during their existence, applying sectarian methods against other individual writers and groups. By proclaiming the slogan 'Ally or enemy', Rapp set the authors belonging to the party against those outside it.
Akhrr (*Assotsiatsiya khudozhnikov revolyutsionnoy Rossii*; Association of the Artists of Revolutionary Russia) was founded in 1922 and existed until 1932. At the first congress of the Association in May 1928, its name was changed to Akhr (*Assotsiatsiya khudozhnikov revolutsionii*; Association of Artists of the Revolution). This change was necessary because by that time the association had become a federal organ and spread outside Russia proper.
Its members tried to revive realistic painting particularly genre painting, as practised by the Peredvizhniks: 'We present our everyday life: the Red Army and the life of the workers, peasantry and heroes of the revolution and socialist labour', says a pamphlet issued by Akhrr. The majority of the paintings and drawings which figured at the Akhrr exhibitions were naturalistic and of a low artistic level. Many well-known Soviet painters were members of Akhrr or participants in its exhibitions, including Maskov, Lentulov, Lanseray and Petrov-Vodkin, members of the former Knave of Diamonds and *Mir Iskusstva* groups.

27 Quoted from *V. Mayakovsky v vospominaniyakh sovremennikov* (*V. Mayakovsky in the Recollections of his Contemporaries*), Moscow, 1963, p. 367.

28 *Molodaya Gvardiya* (*Young Guard*); *Sputnik Kommunista* (*The Communist's Fellow-traveller*); *Sovietskoe Kino* (*Soviet Film*); *Radioslushatel* (*Radio Listener*); *Za Rubezhom* (*Beyond our Borders*, a foreign affairs review).

29 The debate was held in the Moscow Polytechnic Museum following the appearance of Polonsky's article in *Izvestia*, entitled 'Lef or bluff?' The article attacked the theory and practice of the Lef group, and Polonsky made sarcastic remarks about 'the letters of one obscure Rodchenko'. The phrase refers to the letters the artist wrote home from Paris, parts of which were published in the first number of *Novii Lef* in 1927.

30 Quoted from: *Novoe o Mayakovskom,* (*New Data on Mayakovsky*), Moscow, 1958, p. 54.

31 The 'propedeutic' (preparatory or introductory) course first figured in the Bauhaus syllabus. Specialization was preceded by an obligatory introductory subject designed to acquaint the students with the fundamentals of form creation in art. It gave them a certain knowledge of the fields of analytical drawing, abstract elements of form, and the examination and artistic formulation of material. The preparatory course at the Bauhaus, unlike the one at Vkhutemas, lasted only one term.

32 Aviakhim: a voluntary social organization formed by Soviet citizens in 1925 to strengthen the country's defences and promote the development of its industry.

33 Ripolin: an enamel paint.

34 In his *Concise History of Modern Sculpture*, Herbert Read erroneously mentions Rodchenko as one of the Soviet artists who in 1922 visited Berlin on the occasion of the Russian Arts and Applied Arts exhibition there.

35 Rodchenko's work as a photographic artist is reviewed by L. Volkov-Lannit in his *Alexander Rodchenko* (Moscow, 1968) and by L. Linhart in his *Alexander Rodčenko* (Prague, 1964).

36 *Oktyabr* (October): an art society formed in 1928 by artists, architects, film experts and art historians. Its founding members included Alexander Vesnin, Victor Vesnin, Alexei Gan, Alexander Deineka, Gustav Klutsis, Dimitri Moor, Sergei Eisenstein, Béla Uitz and Diego Rivera. One of the important points in its programme was replacement of easel painting by Productivist art. However, the society was not able to give effective support to the artists who endeavoured to put Productivist ideas into practice. In 1931 October was dissolved and many of its members joined Rapkh (*Rossiyskaya Assotsiatsiya Proletarskikh Khudozhikov*; Russian Association of Proletarian Artists).

The 1930 programme of the photogaphy section of the October group included the following: 'We definitely reject every representation that tends to distort the essence of photography and that underrates reality. ... We reject the practice of Akhr, their demurely smiling pretty little faces, smoking chimneys, and the *kvass*-sodden patriotism of workers uniformly shown with sickle and hammer. ... We reject the bourgeois concept of 'new form' and 'Leftist photography', which came to us from the West. We reject the aesthetics of Mancel and Moholy-Nagy's abstract 'Leftist' photography. ... Photography, superseding the obsolete techniques of old spatial art, will play an immensely important role in the development of proletarian art.'

From an application to Rapkh filed by a number of members of the group in 1931: 'The management of October has abandoned the social struggle to strengthen the position of Productivist art and seeks to replace it with abstract theoretics and leave the artists without support and guidance in their practical work. We, members of the Productivist group of the society, have therefore decided ... to apply for our admission to Rapkh. (Signed) A. Deineka, G. Klutsis, P. Freiburg, S. Senkin, N. Pinug, V. Kulagina, V. Yolkin.

37 Goznak: State Banknote Issuing Office.

38 *Prozhektor* (*Projector*); *Krasnoye Studenchestvo* (*Red Students*); *Dayosh* (approx.: *Go ahead!*); *Borba klassov* (*Class Struggle*).

39 Goelro (*Gosudarstvennaya komissiya po elektrifikatsii Rossii* (State Committee for the Electrification of Russia): established in 1920.

40 This is probably a reference to László Moholy-Nagy's book *Malerei, Fotografie, Film* (Munich, 1925, Bauhausbücher No. 8).

Select bibliography

ABRAMOVA. A. 'A. M. Rodchenko'. *Iskusstvo*, No. 11, 1966.

ARVATOV, B. *Agit i proiskusstvo* (*Propagandistic and Productivist Art*). Moscow, 1930.

ARVATOV, B. *Iskusstvo i proizvodstvo* (*Art and Production*). Moscow, 1926.

BUSH, M., A. Zamoshkin. *Puty sovietskoy zhivopisy 1917–1932* (*The Road of Soviet Painting 1917–1932*). Moscow, 1933.

CHICHAGOVA, G. D. 'A. M. Rodchenko', 1965. Manuscript.

DE MICHELI, M. *Az avantgardizmus* (*Avant-Gardism*). Gondolat, Budapest, 1969.

GAN, A. *Konstruktivizm* (*Constructivism*). Tver, 1922.

GRAY, C. *The Russian Experiment in Art : 1863–1922.* London and New York, 1962.

KHARDZHIYEV, N. *A. M. Rodchenko. Iskusstvo knigi* (*Book Art*). Volume 2. Moscow, 1961, pp. 189–192.

LAPSHIN, V. 'Zhizny, polnaya poiskov' (In Pursuit of Discoveries). *Tvorchestvo*, No. 9, 1962.

Lef, 1923–1925, and *Novii Lef*, 1927–1928.

LINHART, L. *Alexander Rodčenko.* Prague, 1964.

LYAKHOV, V. *Sovietsky reklamny plakat 1917–1932* (*The Soviet Advertisement Poster 1917–1932*). Moscow, 1972.

READ, H. *A Concise History of Modern Painting.* London and New York, 1959–74.

READ, H. *A Concise History of Modern Sculpture.* London and New York, 1964.

RODCHENKO, A. M. 'Liniya' (The Line), 1921. Manuscript.

RODCHENKO, A. M. 'O Vladimire Tatline' (On Vladimir Tatlin), after 1940. Manuscript.

RODCHENKO, A. M. 'Rabota s Mayakovskym' (My Work With Mayakovsky),1940. Manuscript.

Sovietskoe iskusstvo za 15 let. Materiali i dokumenty (*Fifteen years of Soviet Fine Art, Documents*). Edited by I. Matsa, L. Reingerndt and L. Rempely, Moscow, 1933.

STRIZHENOVA, T. *Iz istoriy sovietskovo kostyuma* (*From the History of Soviet Dress Design*). Moscow, 1972.

TARABUKIN, N. *Ot molberta k mashinye* (*From the Easel to the Machine*). Moscow, 1923.

UMANSKY, K. *Neue Kunst in Russland, 1914–1919.* (*New Art in Russia, 1914–1919*). Potsdam and Munich, 1920.

VOLKOV-LANNIT, L. *Alexander Rodchenko.* Moscow, 1968.

ZHADOVA, L. 'A. M. Rodchenko'. *Lettres Françaises*, 10 November 1966.

Exhibitions

1913 Second Periodic Exhibition of the Kazan School of Arts. Kazan.
1913 Third Periodic Exhibition. Kazan.
1914 Exhibition. Perm.
1914 Fifth Exhibition. Ryazan.
1916 Fourth Exhibition of Pictures and Sculpture. Moscow.
1916 'The Store'. Futurist exhibition. Moscow.
1918 First Exhibition of the Painters' Trade Union. Moscow.
1918 Exhibition of the Trade Union of New Artists. Moscow.
1918 Exhibition of the Leftist Federation of Painters. Club of the Leftist Federation. Moscow.
1918 'Five Years of Art'. Rodchenko's one-man show in the club of the Leftist Federation. Moscow.
1919 Fifth State Exhibition staged by the Commissariat of Education. ('From Impressionism to Non-Objective painting'.) Moscow.
1919 Tenth State Exhibition staged by the Commissariat of Education. ('Non-Objective art and Suprematism'.) Moscow.
1919 Eleventh State Exhibition. Moscow.
1919 Third Exhibition of Paintings. Ryazan.
1919 First State Exhibition of Local and Moscow Artists. Vitebsk.
1920 Nineteenth State Exhibition staged by the Commissariat of Education. Moscow.
1920 Exhibition organized to celebrate the Third Congress of the Communist International. Moscow.
1920 Zhivskulptura (Painting and Sculpture) Exhibition. Moscow.
1920 Second Fine Arts Exhibition. Sovietsk.
1920 First Fine Arts Exhibition. Kozmodiemyansk.
1920 First State Exhibition ('Art and Science'). Kazan.
1921 Second Obmokhu Spring Exhibition. Moscow.
1921 Third Obmokhu Exhibition. Moscow.
1921 '5 × 5 = 25' Exhibition. Moscow.
1921 Third Fine Arts Exhibition. Sovietsk.
1922 First Russian Fine Arts Exhibition. Berlin.
1923 'Five Years of Stage Design'. Moscow.
1924 Fourteenth Bienniale. Venice.
1925 First Film Poster Exhibition. Moscow.
1925 Third Exhibition of Kaluga and Moscow artists. Kaluga.
1925 'Arts décoratifs'. Paris International Applied Arts Exhibition.
1926 Second Film Poster Exhibition. Moscow.
1926 Exhibition of Theatrical Art staged by the National Institute for Cultural Relations. New York.
1927 National Graphic Exhibition. Moscow.
1927 Press Exhibition organized by the Commissariat of Education. Leipzig.
1927 'Ten Years of Russian Xylography'. Leningrad.
1928 'Ten Years of Russian Graphic Art'. Moscow.
1928 'Ten Years of Soviet Photo-Art'. Moscow, Leningrad.
1928 Eighth International Photographic Exhibition. New York, Westminster (Canada).
1929 'The results of the 1928–29 Moscow theatrical season'. Moscow.
1929 First Exhibition of the Moscow Stage Designers' Union. Moscow.
1929 'Soviet Graphic Art'. Kuybishev.

1929 Photo Exhibition organized by the Society of Film Fans. Moscow.
1929 First Chicago International Photographic Season.
1929 First International Photographic Exhibition, Vienna.
1929 'Film und Foto'. Stuttgart, Berlin.
1929 'Revolutionary and Social Programme'. Moscow.
1930 Exhibition of the Photo Department of the October artists' union. Moscow.
1930 'V. V. Mayakovsky's 20 Years of Work'. Moscow.
1930 Graphic Exhibition. Perm.
1931 International Book Art Exhibition. Paris.
1931 Exhibition of the Photo Section of the October artists' union. Moscow.
1931 Photomontage. Berlin.
1932 V. V. Mayakovsky exhibition. Literary Museum. Moscow.
1932 Soviet Art Exhibition. Königsberg.
1933 'The Construction of the Moscow-Volga Canal'. Dmitrov.
1933 Fifteen years of art in the 'RSFSR'. Moscow.
1933 Soviet Graphic Art, Book, Poster and Photo Exhibition. Marseille.
1933 'Soviet Art Today'. San Francisco, Chicago, Philadelphia.
1934 Exhibition of the Polish Photo Society. Warsaw.
1935 Exhibition of Masters of Soviet Photographic Art. Moscow.
1935 'Seventeen Years of Soviet Stage Design'. Moscow.
1936 International 'Manes' Photo Salon. Prague.
1937 Thirty-second International Photo Salon. Paris.
1937 Soviet Pavilion at the Paris World Exhibition (journals on show).
1938 First Federal Photographic Exhibition. Moscow, Leningrad.
1938 Soviet Photographic Exhibition. Kaunas (Lithuania).
1939 Twelfth International 'Iris' Photo Salon. Antwerp.
1939 Photo Exhibition dedicated to the Eighteenth Party Congress.
1939 Sixth International Photo Salon. Charleroi.
1939 V. V. Mayakovsky Exhibition. Sochi.
1939 Photo Exhibition in the Writers' Club. Moscow.
1939 Soviet Pavilion at the New York World's Fair (journals on show).
1940 Eighth Photo Art Exhibition. Zagreb.
1948 First Book Art Exhibition. Moscow.
1950 Book Art Exhibition organized by Glavizdat. Moscow.
1955 Photographic Art Exhibition. Moscow.
1957 First posthumous exhibition. Journalists' Centre. Moscow.
1957 Soviet Revolutionary Posters. Warsaw.
1958 Photographic Art in the Soviet Union. Moscow.
1961 Exhibition for Rodchenko's seventieth birthday. Moscow Writers' Centre.
1962 A.M. Rodchenko Exhibition (photography, books, graphic art, posters). Leningrad Writers' Centre.
1962 Exhibition at the A.M. Rodchenko memorial evening in the State Literary Museum. Moscow.
1964 '125 Years of Photography'. Film Artists' Centre. Moscow.
1965 The Russian Theatre in the 1920s. Milan.
1965 Photo Art Exhibition, Czechoslovak State Literary and Art Publishers. Prague.
1967 'My Moscow' – jubilee photo exhibition. Moscow.
1967 International Revolutionary Poster Design 1917–1967. Warsaw.
1967 Eastern European avant—garde 1910–1930. Berlin.
1968 A.M. Rodchenko Exhibition. Moscow Journalists' Centre.
1970 A.M. Rodchenko Exhibition. Kostroma.
1971 'Art and Revolution'. Soviet Art and Decoration from 1917. London.
1971 A.M. Rodchenko Exhibition. Museum of Modern Art. New York.

List of illustrations

42 *Two Figures*. 1919. Oil on veneer. 149.5 × 97 cm (58.8 × 38.2 in).
   Former George Costakis Collection, Moscow.
43 *Abstract Drawing*. 1921. Pencil on paper. 18.3 × 14 cm (7.2 × 5.5 in).
44 *Lino-cut*. 1918. 15.5 × 10.5 cm (6.1 × 4.1 in).
45 *Lino-cut*. 1918. 15.5 × 10.5 cm (6.1 × 4.1 in).
46 *Lino-cut*. 1918. 19.5 × 15 cm (7.7 × 5.9 in).
47 *Line Composition*. 1918. Pencil on tracing paper. 37 × 24 cm (14.6 × 9.4 in).
48 *Page from a Notebook*. 1919.
49 *Line Composition*. 1919. Pencil on paper. 17.3 × 11.7 cm (6.8 × 4.6 in).
50 *Line Composition*. 1919. Pencil on paper. 29 × 23 cm (11.4 × 9.1 in).
51 *Line Composition*. 1919. Pencil on paper. 35 × 20 cm (13.8 × 7.9 in).
52 *Composition*. 1919. Ink on paper.
53 *Circles and Straight Lines*. 1920. Coloured ink on paper. 32 × 19.7 cm
   (12.6 × 7.8 in).
54 *Circles and Straight Lines*. 1920. Coloured ink on paper. 32.3 × 20 cm
   (12.7 × 7.9 in).
55 *Line Composition*. 1921. Pencil on paper. 35.5 × 22 cm (14 × 8.7 in).
56 *Construction*. 1918.
57 *Construction*. 1918.
58 *Construction*. 1918.
59 *Construction*. 1918.
60 *Construction*. 1918.
61 *Construction*. 1918.
62 *Spatial Construction*. 1920.
63 *Spatial Construction*. 1920.
64 *Spatial Construction*. 1920.
65 *Hanging Construction*. 1920.
66 *Hanging Construction*. 1920.
67 *Hanging Construction*. 1920.
68 *Hanging Construction*. 1920.
69 *Lamp for the Café Pittoresque*. 1917. Ink on paper. 26.5 × 20.5 cm (10.4 × 8.1 in).
70 *Lamp for the Café Pittoresque*. 1917. Pencil on paper. 26.5 × 20.5 cm
   (10.4 × 8.1 in).
71 *Lamp for the Café Pittoresque*. 1917. Crayon on paper. 26.5 × 20.5 cm
   (10.4 × 8.1 in).
72 *News Kiosk*. 1919. Ink and tempera on paper. 50 × 34 cm (19.7 × 13.4 in).
73 *Airport*. 1918. Ink on paper. 35 × 22 cm (13.8 × 8.7 in).
74 *Building*. 1920. Coloured ink on paper. 20.8 × 26 cm (8.2 × 10.2 in).
75 *Emblem*. 1925.
76 *Emblem*. 1925.
77 *Perpetuum Mobile*. 1921. Pencil on paper. 35.5 × 22 cm (14 × 8.7 in).
78 *Tray*. 1922. Ink and gouache on paper. 58 × 45 cm (22.8 × 17.7 in).
79 *Teacups and Tray*. 1922. Ink and tempera on paper. 37 × 27 cm (14.6 × 10.6 in).
80 *Advertisement*. 1924.
81 *Trade Mark for Dobrolyet*. 1923
82 *Poster*. 1923.
83 *Trade Mark for Mosselprom*. 1923.
84 *Poster*. 1923.
85 *Poster*. 1923.
86 *Poster*. 1923.
87 *Poster*. 1923.
88
   Sweet-wrappers. 1923.
–89
90 *Poster*. 1923.
91 *Poster*. 1923.
92 *Poster*. 1923.
93 *Poster*. 1923.
94 *Poster*. 1923.
95 *Poster*. 1923.
96 *Advertisement*. 1924. Coloured ink on card. 13 × 13 cm (5.1 × 5.1 in).
97 *Advertisement*. 1924. Coloured ink on card. 12.2 × 9.9 cm (4.8 × 3.9 in).
98 *Advertisement*. 1924.

Index